LA-3B

### Zaner-Bloser
# Handwriting
**With continuous-stroke alphabet**

D1609584

## Author
Clinton S. Hackney

## Contributing Authors
Pamela J. Farris
Janice T. Jones
Linda Leonard Lamme

**Zaner-Bloser, Inc.,** P.O. Box 16764, Columbus, Ohio 43216-6764    1-800-421-3018

Copyright © 1999 Zaner-Bloser, Inc.    ISBN 0-88085-956-3

Developed by Kirchoff/Wohlberg, Inc., in cooperation with Zaner-Bloser Publishers

Printed in the United States of America

00 01 02 WC 5 4

You already know handwriting is important.
Now take a look at...

**NEW SIMPLIFIED**

# Zaner-Bloser Handwriting

## Easier to read! Easier to write! Easier to teach!

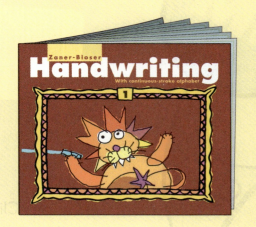

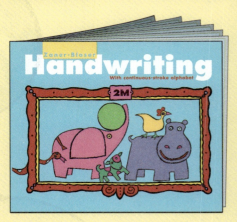

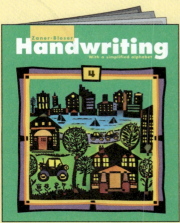

I see Zaner-Bloser's alphabet in the books I read.

I like Zaner-Bloser because it's so easy to write.

Zaner-Bloser's new program is easy to teach.

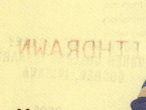

You already know handwriting is important, but did you know...

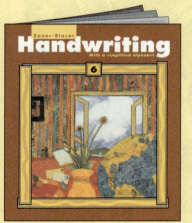

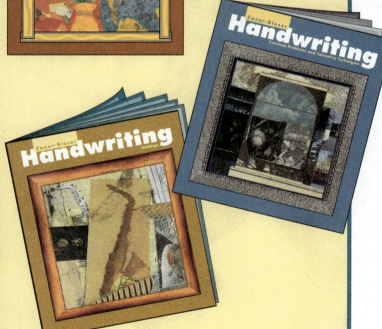

## Did You Know...

Annually, the U.S. Postal Service receives 38 million illegibly addressed letters, costing American taxpayers $4 million each year.

–*American Demographics*, Dec. 1992

## Did You Know...

Hundreds of thousands of tax returns are delayed every year because figures, notes, and signatures are illegible.

–*Better Handwriting in 30 Days*, 1989

## Did You Know...

Poor handwriting costs American business $200 million annually.

–*American Demographics*, Dec. 1992

# Zaner-Bloser's CONTINUOUS-STROKE manuscript alphabet

Aa Bb Cc Dd Ee Ff Gg
Oo Pp Qq Rr Ss Tt

## Easier to Read

Our vertical manuscript alphabet is like the alphabet kids see every day inside and outside of the classroom. They see it in their school books, in important environmental print like road signs, and in books and cartoons they read for fun.

"[Slanted] manuscript is not only harder to learn than traditional [vertical] print, but it creates substantially more letter recognition errors and causes more letter confusion than does the traditional style."

—Debby Kuhl and Peter Dewitz in a paper presented at the 1994 meeting of the American Educational Research Association

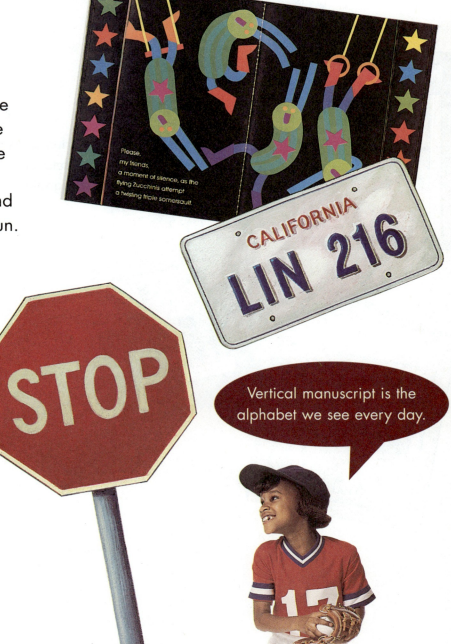

CALIFORNIA LIN 216

STOP

Vertical manuscript is the alphabet we see every day.

# Hh Ii Jj Kk Ll Mm Nn
# Uu Vv Ww Xx Yy Zz

## Easier to Write

Our vertical manuscript alphabet is written with continuous strokes— fewer pencil lifts—so there's a greater sense of flow in writing. And kids can write every letter once they learn four simple strokes that even kindergartners can manage.

*Four simple strokes: circle, horizontal line, vertical line, slanted line*

"The writing hand has to change direction more often when writing the [slanted] alphabet, do more retracing of lines, and make more strokes that occur later in children's development."

–Steve Graham in *Focus on Exceptional Children*, 1992

Many kids can already write their names when they start school (vertical manuscript).

### Kirk

Why should they have to relearn them in another form (slanted manuscript)? With Zaner-Bloser, they don't have to.

### Kirk

## Easier to Teach

Our vertical manuscript alphabet is easy to teach because there's no reteaching involved. Children are already familiar with our letterforms—they've seen them in their environment and they've learned them at home.

"Before starting school, many children learn how to write traditional [vertical] manuscript letters from their parents or preschool teachers. Learning a special alphabet such as [slanted] means that these children will have to relearn many of the letters they can already write."

–Steve Graham in *Focus on Exceptional Children*, 1992

*Aa Bb Cc Dd Ee Ff Gg*
*Nn Oo Pp Qq Rr Ss*

## Simplified letterforms...
## Easier to read and write

old letterform

Letterforms are simplified so they're easier to write and easier to identify in writing. The new simplified **Q** now looks like a **Q** instead of a number 2.

old letterform

Our simplified letterforms use the headline, midline, and baseline as a guide for where letters start and stop. The new simplified **d** touches the headline instead of stopping halfway.

old letterform

No more "cane stems!" Our new simplified letterforms begin with a small curve instead of fancy loops that can be difficult for students to write.

*Hh Ii Jj Kk Ll Mm*
*Tt Uu Vv Ww Xx Yy Zz*

## Simplified letterforms...
### Easier to teach

When handwriting is easy for students to write, instruction time is cut way back! That's the teaching advantage with Zaner-Bloser Handwriting. Our cursive letterforms are simplified so instead of spending a lot of time teaching fancy loops that give kids trouble, teachers give instruction for simple, basic handwriting that students can use for the rest of their lives.

And remember, with Zaner-Bloser Handwriting, students learn to write manuscript with continuous strokes. That means that when it's time for those students to begin writing cursive, the transition comes naturally because they already know the flow of continuous strokes.

These simple letters are so much easier to teach!

# The Student Edition...set up for student success

**Uppercase and lowercase letterforms are taught together.**

**Letter models with arrows show stroke direction and sequence.**

**Students trace models first before writing on their own.**

b B    p P    r R

Trace and write the letters.

b b b b b b        B B B B B

p p p p p p        P P P P P

r r r r r r        R R R R R

**Circle your best letters.**

**My Own Words**

32

**Grade 2M Student Edition**

*Language arts connections are easy with activities like this one. Here, students learn how to use quotation marks as they practice their handwriting.*

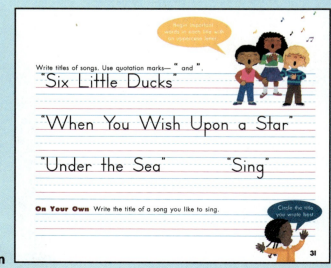

Write titles of songs. Use quotation marks— " and ".

"Six Little Ducks"

"When You Wish Upon a Star"

"Under the Sea"    "Sing"

**On Your Own** Write the title of a song you like to sing.

*Circle the title you wrote best.*

31

**Grade 2M Student Edition**

Relevant practice teaches students language skills, such as how to write titles.

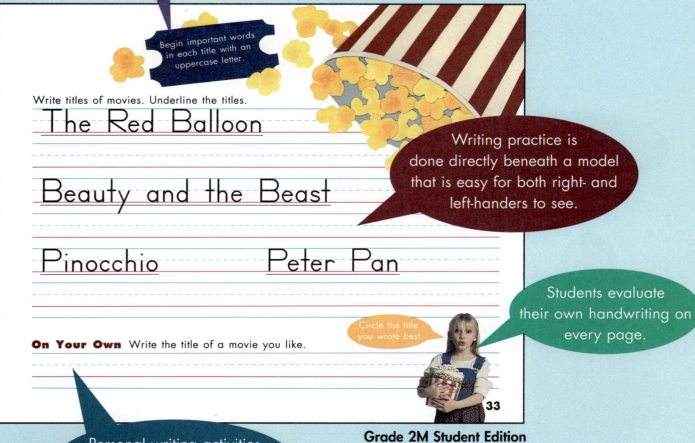

Begin important words in each title with an uppercase letter.

Write titles of movies. Underline the titles.

The Red Balloon

Beauty and the Beast

Pinocchio          Peter Pan

**On Your Own** Write the title of a movie you like.

Circle the title you wrote best

Writing practice is done directly beneath a model that is easy for both right- and left-handers to see.

Students evaluate their own handwriting on every page.

33

**Grade 2M Student Edition**

Personal writing activities help make language arts connections.

*Activities like this one, in which students write the word "bread" in different languages, offer teachers the opportunity to bring multiculturalism into the classroom.*

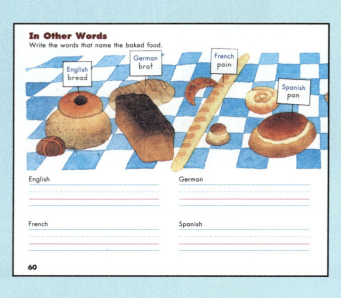

**In Other Words**
Write the words that name the baked food.

English bread

German brot

French pain

Spanish pan

English

German

French

Spanish

60

**Grade 2M Student Edition**

# The Teacher Edition...streamlined instruction

At-a-glance stroke descriptions are short and easy to find.

Fun activities motivate students to learn.

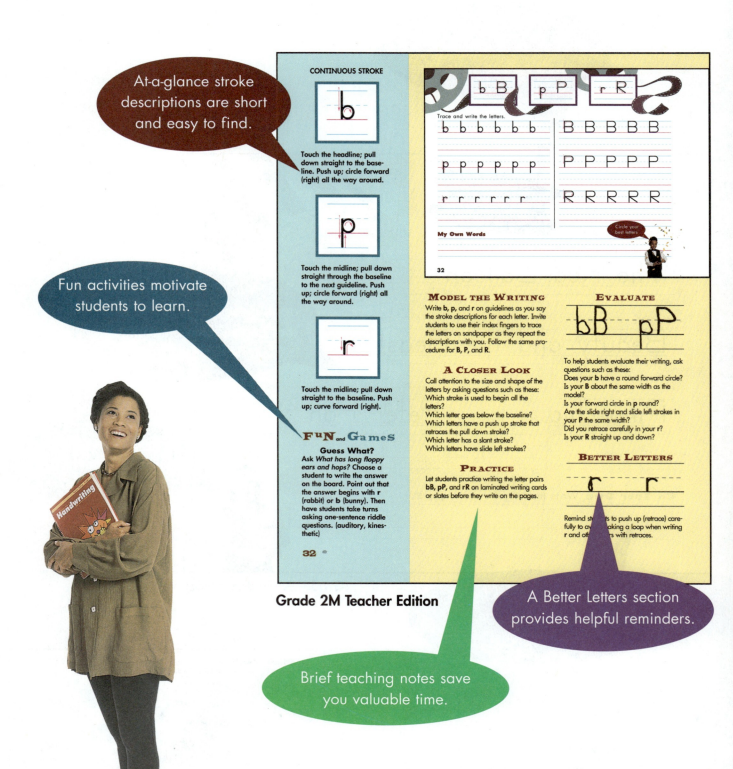

**CONTINUOUS STROKE**

Touch the headline; pull down straight to the baseline. Push up; circle forward (right) all the way around.

Touch the midline; pull down straight through the baseline to the next guideline. Push up; circle forward (right) all the way around.

Touch the midline; pull down straight to the baseline. Push up; curve forward (right).

### FᵁN and Games
**Guess What?**
Ask *What has long floppy ears and hops?* Choose a student to write the answer on the board. Point out that the answer begins with **r** (rabbit) or **b** (bunny). Then have students take turns asking one-sentence riddle questions. (auditory, kinesthetic)

32

**Trace and write the letters.**

b b b b b    B B B B B

p p p p p    P P P P P

r r r r r    R R R R R

**My Own Words**

*Circle your best letters*

32

### MODEL THE WRITING
Write **b**, **p**, and **r** on guidelines as you say the stroke descriptions for each letter. Invite students to use their index fingers to trace the letters on sandpaper as they repeat the descriptions with you. Follow the same procedure for **B**, **P**, and **R**.

### A CLOSER LOOK
Call attention to the size and shape of the letters by asking questions such as these:
Which stroke is used to begin all the letters?
Which letter goes below the baseline?
Which letters have a push up stroke that retraces the pull down stroke?
Which letter has a slant stroke?
Which letters have slide left strokes?

### PRACTICE
Let students practice writing the letter pairs **bB**, **pP**, and **rR** on laminated writing cards or slates before they write on the pages.

### EVALUATE

To help students evaluate their writing, ask questions such as these:
Does your **b** have a round forward circle?
Is your **B** about the same width as the model?
Is your forward circle in **p** round?
Are the slide right and slide left strokes in your **P** the same width?
Did you retrace carefully in your **r**?
Is your **R** straight up and down?

### BETTER LETTERS

Remind students to push up (retrace) carefully to avoid making a loop when writing **r** and other letters with retraces.

**Grade 2M Teacher Edition**

A Better Letters section provides helpful reminders.

Brief teaching notes save you valuable time.

x

The student page is close to the instruction for that page.

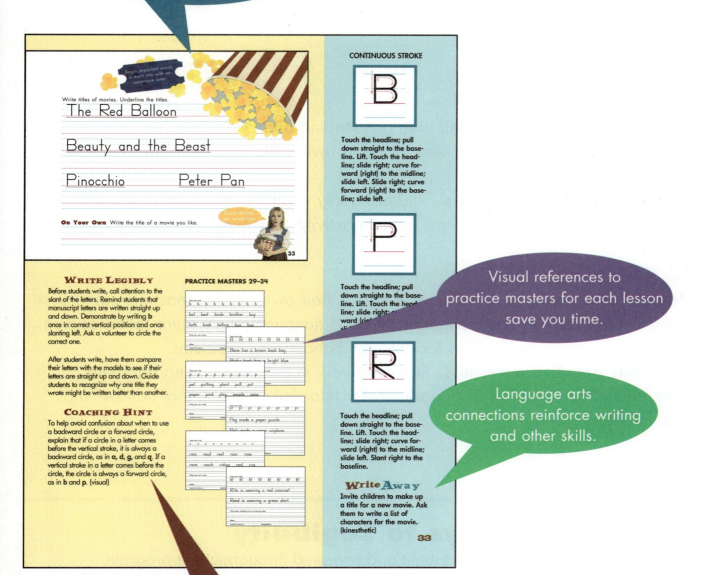

**Grade 2M Teacher Edition**

Coaching Hints offer insight and additional information.

Visual references to practice masters for each lesson save you time.

Language arts connections reinforce writing and other skills.

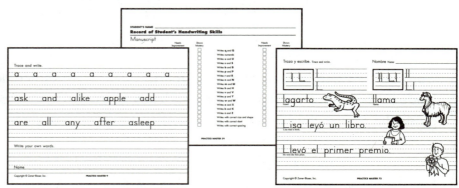

**Grade 2M Practice Masters**

*An accompanying book of practice masters offers additional practice for every letter and skill students learn. It also includes resources to make teaching easier—certificates, an evaluation record, letters to send home to keep parents and guardians involved, and Spanish activities.*

# Evaluation and Assessment...
# consistent guidance throughout the year

## Student self-evaluation...

**In every lesson.** Students evaluate their own handwriting and circle their best work.

**In every review.** Six times during the year, students review the letterforms they've learned and again evaluate their handwriting.

**Through relevant practice activities.** Students apply what they've learned in personal writing and other relevant practice activities. In each activity, they evaluate their handwriting.

## Teacher assessment...

**In every lesson and review.** As students evaluate their own writing, teachers can assess their letterforms, as well as their comprehension of good handwriting. A Better Letters section for each lesson offer teachers helpful hints for common handwriting problems.

**Through relevant practice activities.** Students' work in personal writing and other relevant practice activities offers lots of opportunity for informal assessment of handwriting, language arts, and other areas.

---

## The Keys to Legibility

These four Keys to Legibility are taught and reviewed throughout the program.
They remind children that their goal should be legible handwriting.

### Size

Consistently sized letters are easy to read. Students learn to use midlines and headlines to guide the size of their letters.

### Slant

Vertical letters are easier to read. Students learn how to position their papers and hold their pencils so writing vertical letters comes with ease.

### Shape

Four simple strokes—circle, horizontal line, vertical line, and slanted line—make it easy for students to write letters with consistent and proper shape.

### Spacing

Correct spacing between letters and words makes handwriting easy to read. Practical hints show students how to determine correct spacing.

**On Your Own**

If you dressed like a clown, what would you look like?
Draw a picture and describe it.

This is me
dressed like
a silly clown.
I have a funny
hat and big
floppy shoes.

**Completed Grade 2M
Student Edition**

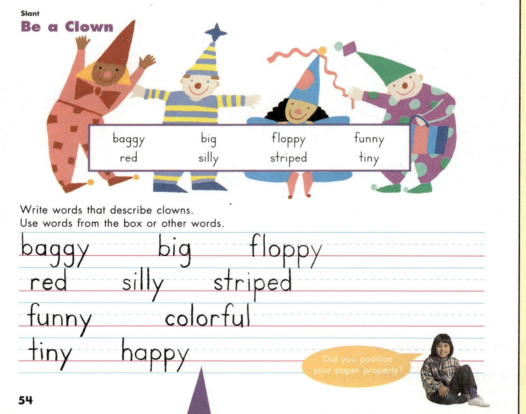

Slant
**Be a Clown**

| baggy | big | floppy | funny |
| red | silly | striped | tiny |

Write words that describe clowns.
Use words from the box or other words.

baggy      big      floppy
red      silly      striped
funny      colorful
tiny      happy

Did you position
your paper properly?

54

# A huge collection of supplementary materials... makes handwriting even easier to teach!

**A** **Evaluation Guides** *grades 1–6*

**B** **Poster/Wall Chart Super Pak**
*grades K–6, includes Handwriting Positions Wall Chart, Keys to Legibility Wall Chart, Alphabet Wall Chart, Simplified Stroke Descriptions, and a Portfolio Assessment Guide*

**C** **Story Journals** *grades K–4*

**D** **Manuscript/Cursive Card Set** *grades 1–6*

**E** **Sentence Strips** *grades K–6*

**F** **Writing Journals** *grades 1–6*

**G** **My ABC Journal** *grades K–1*

**H** **Pignic Alphabet Book** *grades K–2*

**I** **From Anne to Zach Alphabet Book** *grades K–2*

**J** **Letter Cards** *grades K–2*

**K** **Manuscript/Cursive Fonts**

**L** **Manuscript Kin-Tac Cards** *grades K–2*

For more information about these materials, call 1-800-421-3018.

# Vertical vs. *Slanted* Manuscript

## What the research shows

Using a slanted alphabet has been a trend in handwriting instruction. It's actually not a new development—the first slanted alphabet was created in 1968. A sort of bridge between manuscript and cursive, this slanted alphabet used unconnected letterforms like the traditional vertical manuscript, but its letterforms were slanted like cursive.

It seemed like a good idea. This alphabet was to be easier to write than cursive, yet similar enough to cursive that children wouldn't learn two *completely* different alphabets. But after several years of use in some schools, research has uncovered some unfortunate findings.

### Slanted manuscript can be difficult to write

Slanted manuscript was created to be similar to cursive, so it uses more complicated strokes such as small curves, and these strokes can be difficult for young children.

Vertical manuscript, on the other hand, is consistent with the development of young children. Each of its letters is formed with simple strokes—straight lines, circles, and slanted lines. One researcher found that the strokes used in vertical manuscript are the same as the shapes children use in their drawings (Farris, 1993). Because children are familiar with these shapes, they can identify and form the strokes with little difficulty.

### Slanted manuscript can create problems with legibility

Legibility is an important goal in handwriting. Obviously, content should not be sacrificed for legibility, but what is handwriting if it cannot be read?

Educational researchers have tested the legibility of slanted manuscript and found that children writing vertical manuscript "performed significantly better" than those writing slanted manuscript. The writers of the slanted alphabet tended to make more misshapen letterforms, tended to extend their strokes above and below the guidelines, and had a difficult time keeping their letterforms consistent in size (Graham, 1992).

On the other hand, the vertical manuscript style of print has a lot of support in the area of research. Advertisers have known for years that italic type has a lower readability rate than vertical "roman" type. Research shows that in 30 minute readings, the italic style is read 4.9% slower than roman type (14–16 words per minute). This is why most literature, especially literature for early readers, is published using roman type.

### Slanted manuscript can impair letter recognition

Educators have suspected that it would be beneficial for students to write and read the same style of alphabet. In other words, if children *read* vertical manuscript, they should also *write* vertical manuscript. Now it has been found that inconsistent alphabets may actually be detrimental to children's learning.

Researchers have found that slanted manuscript impairs the ability of some young children to recognize many letters. Some children who learn the slanted style alphabet find it difficult to recognize many of the traditional letterforms they see in books and environmental print. "[These children] consistently had difficulty identifying several letters, often making the same erroneous response to the same letter," the researchers reported. They concluded that slanted manuscript "creates substantially more letter recognition errors and causes more letter confusion than does the traditional style." (Kuhl & Dewitz, 1994).

> *"…slanted manuscript letters cannot be recommended as a replacement for the traditional manuscript alphabet."*

### Slanted manuscript does not help with transition

One of the benefits proposed by the creators of the slanted manuscript alphabet was that it made it easier for children to make the transition from manuscript to cursive writing. However, no difference in transition time has been found between the two styles of manuscript alphabets. In addition, the slanted style does not seem to enhance young children's production of cursive letters (Graham, 1992).

The slanted style of manuscript appeared to be a good idea. But educators should take a close look at what the research shows before adopting this style of alphabet. As one researcher has said, "Given the lack of supportive evidence and the practical problems involved in implementation, slanted manuscript letters cannot be recommended as a replacement for the traditional manuscript alphabet" (Graham, 1994).

Farris, P.J. (1993). Learning to write the ABC's: A comparison of D'Nealian and Zaner-Bloser handwriting styles. *Indiana Reading Quarterly*, 25 (4), 26–33.

Graham, S. (1992). Issues in handwriting instruction. *Focus on Exceptional Children*, 25 (2).

Graham, S. (1994, Winter). Are slanted manuscript alphabets superior to the traditional manuscript alphabet? *Childhood Education*, 91–95.

Kuhl, D. & Dewitz, P. (1994, April). The effect of handwriting style on alphabet recognition. Paper presented at the annual meeting of the American Educational Research Association, New Orleans, LA.

# Under your care . . .
## your students receive the best possible attention everyday!

Now that you use *Zaner-Bloser Handwriting,* we want to be sure you get the attention you need to make your job more successful. We have many communication channels available to meet your needs: phone our Customer Service Department at 1-800-421-3018, visit our website at www.zaner-bloser.com, use the card below to write to our editors, and use the card at the bottom to join our Customer Care Club.

# Zaner-Bloser cares!

If you have any questions or comments concerning Zaner-Bloser instructional materials or questions about the teaching of handwriting, you may use this card to write to us. We will be happy to assist you in any way possible.

_____

_____

_____

_____

_____

| Ms., Mr., etc. | Name | Position | Grade Level(s) |
|---|---|---|---|
| School | | School Address | |
| City | | State | ZIP |
| ( ) School Telephone | | ( ) After Hours Phone | ( ) FAX |

MH0327

# Zaner-Bloser Customer Care Club

Join the Zaner-Bloser Customer Care Club and we'll make sure you stay up-to-date on current educational research and products. To enroll, you may return this card or call our Customer Care Club hotline at 1-800-387-2410. Upon enrollment, we'll get you started with a gift of information about teaching handwriting.

 **YES!** Please enroll me in the Zaner-Bloser Customer Care Club and send me the following pamphlet: **The Left-Handed Child in a Right-Handed World**

**Zaner-Bloser**

2200 W. Fifth Ave.
PO Box 16764
Columbus, OH
43216-6764

Visit our website:
www.zaner-bloser.com

| Ms., Mr., etc. | Name | Position | Grade Level(s) |
|---|---|---|---|
| School | | School Address | |
| City | | State | ZIP |
| ( ) School Telephone | | ( ) After Hours Phone | ( ) FAX |

**Please Note: This program is for Zaner-Bloser customers only!**

MH0327

# Zaner-Bloser

Customer Service: 1-800-421-3018

Customer Care Club: 1-800-387-2410

Website: www.zaner-bloser.com

NO POSTAGE
NECESSARY
IF MAILED
IN THE
UNITED STATES

## BUSINESS REPLY MAIL
FIRST CLASS MAIL    PERMIT NO. 295    COLUMBUS, OH

POSTAGE WILL BE PAID BY ADDRESSEE

### Zaner-Bloser
2200 W 5TH AVE
PO BOX 16764
COLUMBUS OH  43272-4176

NO POSTAGE
NECESSARY
IF MAILED
IN THE
UNITED STATES

## BUSINESS REPLY MAIL
FIRST CLASS MAIL    PERMIT NO. 295    COLUMBUS, OH

POSTAGE WILL BE PAID BY ADDRESSEE

### Zaner-Bloser
2200 W 5TH AVE
PO BOX 16764
COLUMBUS OH  43272-4176

# Meeting Students' Individual Handwriting Needs

## The Left-Handed Student

With proper instruction and encouragement, left-handed students can write as well as right-handed students. Three important techniques assist the left-handed student in writing.

### Paper Position

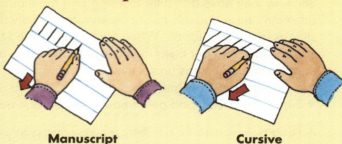

**Manuscript**          **Cursive**

For *manuscript writing,* the **lower right corner** of the paper should point toward the left of the body's mid-section.

For *cursive writing,* the **lower right corner** of the paper should point toward the body's midsection.

Downstrokes are pulled toward the left elbow.

### Pencil Position

The top of the pencil should point toward the left elbow. The pen or pencil should be held at least one inch above the point. This allows students to see what they are writing.

### Arm Position

Holding the left arm close to the body and keeping the hand below the line of writing prevents "hooking" the wrist and smearing the writing.

## Students With Reversal Tendencies

- Downcurve
- Undercurve
- Slant
- Loop forward, undercurve

### Directionality

A problem with directionality (moving from left to right across the page) interferes with a child's ability to form letters correctly and to write text that makes sense. To develop correct directionality, try these techniques:

- Provide opportunities for the child to write at the chalkboard within a confined area with frequent arrows as a reminder of left-to-right progression.
- Prepare sheets of paper on which the left edges and the beginning stroke of a letter, such as *b*, are colored green.

### Letter Reversals

Determine which letters a student most often reverses. Make a list of these reversals and concentrate on them either on an individual basis or by grouping together the students who are reversing the same letters.

- Emphasize each step of the stroke description before the children write a letter.
- Provide a letter for tracing that has been colored according to stroke order. Repeat the stroke description with the children as they write the letter.
- Encourage the children to write the letter as they verbalize the stroke description.

# Students With Other Special Needs

Success in handwriting is almost always a certainty if the initial instruction involves visual, auditory, and kinesthetic stimuli—a multisensory approach. Students need to develop a correct mental and motor image of the stroke, joining, letter, or word before they attempt to write. These techniques may help your students with special needs.

## For the Kinesthetic Learner

- Walk out the letter strokes on the floor.
- Form letters in the air using full-arm movement.
- Make letter models with clay or string.
- Write strokes, letters, and joinings in sand.
- Use different writing instruments, such as crayons, markers, and varied sizes of pencils.
- Trace large strokes, letters, and joinings on the chalkboard and on paper—first with fingers, then with chalk or other media.
- Dip fingers in water and form letters and joinings on the chalkboard.

*Remember that initial instruction, remediation, and maintenance for the student whose primary sensory modality is kinesthetic should be tactile, involving movement and the sense of touch.*

## For the Auditory Learner

- Verbalize each stroke in the letter as that letter is presented.
- Encourage the student to verbalize the letter strokes and to explain how strokes are alike and how they are different in the letterforms.
- Ask students to write random letters as you verbalize the strokes.
- Be consistent in the language you use to describe letters, strokes, shapes, and joinings.

*Students whose primary sensory modality is auditory require instruction that enables them to listen and to verbalize.*

## For the Visual Learner

- Encourage students first to look at the letter as a whole and to ask themselves if the letter is tall or short, fat or skinny. Does all of the letter rest on the baseline, or is it a descender or a tall letter? How many and what kinds of strokes are in the letter?
- Have students look at each individual stroke carefully before they attempt to write the letter.

*As a general rule, a student whose primary sensory modality is visual will have little difficulty in handwriting if instruction includes adequate visual stimuli.*

## For Learners With Attention Deficit Problems

Because they have difficulty focusing and maintaining attention, these students must concentrate on individual strokes in the letterforms. When they have learned the strokes, they can put them together to form letters, and then learn the joinings (in cursive) to write words.
- Give very short assignments.
- Supervise closely and give frequent encouragement.

*Activities recommended for kinesthetic learners are appropriate for students with an attention deficit disorder.*

## General Coaching Tips for Teachers

- Teach a handwriting lesson daily, if possible, for no more than 15 minutes. Short, daily periods of instruction are preferable to longer, but less frequent, periods.
- Surround children with models of good handwriting. Set an example when you write on the chalkboard and on students' papers.
- Teach the letters through basic strokes.
- Emphasize one key to legibility at a time.
- Use appropriately ruled paper. Don't be afraid to increase the size of the grids for any student who is experiencing difficulty.
- Stress comfortable writing posture and pencil position. Increase the size of the pencil for students who "squeeze" the writing implement.
- Show the alternate method of holding the pencil, and allow students to choose the one that is better for them. (Refer to the alternate method shown on the Position Pages in the Teacher Edition.)
- Provide opportunities for children in the upper grades to use manuscript writing. Permit manuscript for some assignments, if children prefer manuscript to cursive.
- Encourage students with poor sustained motor control to use conventional manuscript, with frequent lifts, if continuous manuscript is difficult for them.

Zaner-Bloser
# Handwriting
**With continuous-stroke alphabet**

2M

**Author**
Clinton S. Hackney

**Contributing Authors**
Pamela J. Farris
Janice T. Jones
Linda Leonard Lamme

Zaner-Bloser, Inc.
P.O. Box 16764
Columbus, Ohio 43216-6764

**Teacher Edition Artists:**
Lizi Boyd; Denise & Fernando;
Michael Grejniec; Shari Halpern;
Daniel Moreton; Diane Paterson;
Andy San Diego; Troy Viss
**Photos:**
Stephen Ogilvy

**Author**
Clinton S. Hackney, Ed.D.

**Contributing Authors**
Pamela J. Farris, Ph.D.
Janice T. Jones, M.A.
Linda Leonard Lamme, Ph.D.

**Reviewers**
Judy L. Bausch, Columbus, Georgia
Cherlynn Bruce, Conroe, Texas
Karen H. Burke, Director of Curriculum and Instruction, Bar Mills, Maine
Anne Chamberlin, Lynchburg, Virginia
Carol J. Fuhler, Flagstaff, Arizona
Deborah D. Gallagher, Gainesville, Florida
Kathleen Harrington, Redford, Michigan
Rebecca James, East Greenbush, New York
Gerald R. Maeckelbergh, Principal, Blaine, Minnesota
Bessie B. Peabody, Principal, East St. Louis, Illinois

Marilyn S. Petruska, Coraopolis, Pennsylvania
Sharon Ralph, Nashville, Tennessee
Linda E. Ritchie, Birmingham, Alabama
Roberta Hogan Royer, North Canton, Ohio
Marion Redmond Starks, Baltimore, Maryland
Elizabeth J. Taglieri, Lake Zurich, Illinois
Claudia Williams, Lewisburg, West Virginia

**Credits**
**Art:** Lizi Boyd: 1, 6, 22–23, 28–29, 36–37, 54, 84–85, 99–100; Denise & Fernando: 3–4, 6, 20–21, 34–35, 68–69, 86–87, 100; Gloria Elliott: 5, 16, 42; Michael Grejniec: 4, 7, 11, 24–25, 30–31, 60–61, 76–77, 92–93, 101; Shari Halpern: 3, 6, 26–27, 32–33, 38–39, 44–45, 52, 72–73, 82, 96–97, 100; Daniel Moreton: 43, 53, 71, 81; Diane Paterson: 88–89; Andy San Diego: 3, 4, 6, 46–47, 56–57, 64–65, 80, 100; Troy Viss: 4–5, 7, 16, 42, 48–49, 58–59, 66–67, 74–75, 94–95, 101

**Photos:** John Lei/OPC: 8–9; Stephen Ogilvy: 3–5, 10, 12–19, 23, 26–27, 32–33, 40–43, 45–47, 50, 52, 54–59, 62–63, 68–70, 74–78, 80–87, 90–91, 94–97, 99

**Developed by Kirchoff/Wohlberg, Inc., in cooperation with Zaner-Bloser Publishers**
Cover illustration by Lizi Boyd

ISBN 0-88085-946-6

Copyright © 1999 Zaner-Bloser, Inc.

# CONTENTS

## Getting Started

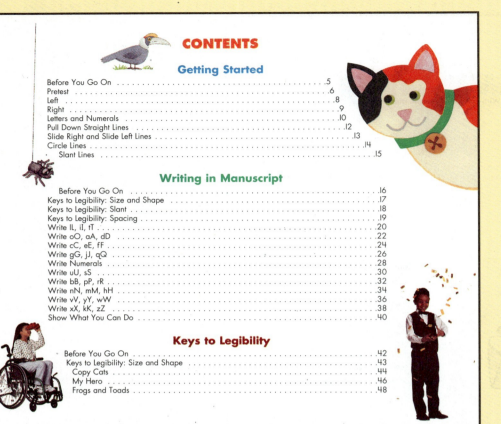

## Writing in Manuscript

## Keys to Legibility

Follow the path. Write each letter you find.

start ➡

finish

What can the letters spell?
Write the word and read the message.

Let's _____.

In this book, you will find letters, words, and sentences to write. You will learn how to make your manuscript writing easy for you and for others to read.

Before You Go On....

5

## HOW THIS BOOK IS ORGANIZED

The **Getting Started** pages will help students learn the vocabulary and conventions of this handwriting program.

In **Writing in Manuscript,** lowercase and uppercase letters are presented together. The letter sequence is determined by common elements of the lowercase letters. Note that models are provided and students have space to write directly beneath the models. **My Own Words** provides an opportunity for students to write familiar words and **On Your Own** encourages them to write about their own experiences.

In the **Keys to Legibility** sections, students apply their handwriting skills. They focus on size and shape, slant, and spacing in order to make their writing legible. These pages include words in several languages.

Point out that students will evaluate their handwriting frequently. Set up a portfolio for each student to assess individual progress throughout the year.

Preview the book with your students. Use this page with your class as an introduction to the Zaner-Bloser handwriting program. Call attention to the letters in the maze and help them figure out the message.

## BOOKS FOR SHARING

*Alphabatty: Riddles From A to Z*
by Ann Walton and Rick Walton

*Eye Spy: A Mysterious Alphabet*
by Linda Bourke

*Anno's Alphabet: An Adventure in Imagination*
by Mitsumasa Anno

*The Z Was Zapped: A Play in Twenty-Six Acts*
by Chris Van Allsburg

*Anno's Counting Book*
by Mitsumasa Anno

*Numblers*
by Suse MacDonald and Bill Oakes

*Sing a Song of Popcorn: Every Child's Book of Poems*
selected by Beatrice S. De Regniers et al.

## BEFORE WRITING

Share the verse on the page with your students. Discuss with students the different kinds of writing they do. Ask them to write the lines of this poem in their best handwriting on the next page.

**Pretest**

I Can
I can write a story.
I can write a poem.
I can write at school,
And I can write at home.

I Can
I can write a story.
I can write a poem.
I can write at school,
And I can write at home.

## I Can

I can write a story.
I can write a poem.
I can write at school,
And I can write at home.

I Can
I can write a story.
I can write a poem.
I can write at school,
And I can write at home.

6

After they write, explain to students that at a future date, they will be asked to write this poem again and compare it with the writing they do today.

Ask students to keep their pretests in their books or writing portfolios for comparison with their posttests later in the year.

## EVALUATE

Observe as students write, and informally assess their present handwriting skills. Then guide them to talk about their writing and to explain why they chose one line of writing as their best.

## I Can

I can write a story.
I can write a poem.
I can write at school,
And I can write at home.

Write the poem in your best handwriting.

Put a star next to your best line of writing.

7

## COACHING HINT

Make a desktop nametag for each student in your class, using tagboard or self-adhesive ruled strips. Tape the nametags to the students' desks so they can use them as writing models. (visual)

### ABCs of Writing Ideas

Discuss with students the various kinds of writing they might do at different times. Brainstorm a list of things they might write. If your students like a challenge, ask them to think of one idea for each letter of the alphabet. Here are some ideas to get started:

> alphabet books
> brochures
> cartoons
> diaries
> envelopes
> friendly letters
> greeting cards

Display the list so students can refer to it often. (visual, auditory)

### Take a Good Look

Take a walk with your class through the classroom or school building. Ask students to look for examples of environmental print. After touring, make a chart of your findings. List the messages and the places where they appeared. Add to this list as students become aware of other print in their environment. (visual)

## BEFORE WRITING

Invite students to play a game of "Simon Says." Give students directions that include the words *left* and *right*. Have them stand facing you. Remind them to follow the direction only when they hear "Simon says." Begin with these:

Simon says, "Touch your head with your right hand."
Touch your nose with your left hand.
Simon says, "Take two giant steps to the left."

Note if any students have difficulty distinguishing left from right.

## Left-Handed Writers

**If you write with your left hand . . .**

Slant your paper. Pull your downstrokes toward your left elbow.

Hold your pencil with your first two fingers and thumb. Point the pencil toward your left elbow.

Sit up tall. Place both arms on the table. Keep your feet flat on the floor.

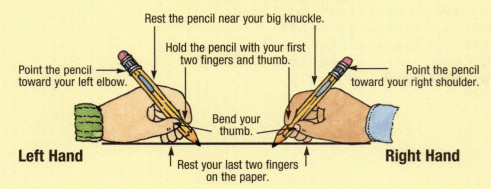

## PENCIL POSITION

Rest the pencil near your big knuckle.

Hold the pencil with your first two fingers and thumb.

Point the pencil toward your left elbow.

Point the pencil toward your right shoulder.

Bend your thumb.

Rest your last two fingers on the paper.

**Left Hand**          **Right Hand**

Work through these pages with the students.

Demonstrate how to place both arms on the desk, with only the elbows off the desk, and how to sit up straight.

Demonstrate the correct way to hold a pencil for both left-handers and right-handers.

Distribute paper with guidelines and help students follow the directions for proper paper position.

## PAPER POSITION

*See the Handwriting Positions Wall Chart for more information.*

## Right-Handed Writers

### If you write with your right hand ...

Keep your paper straight. Pull your downstrokes toward the middle of your body.

Hold your pencil with your first two fingers and thumb. Point the pencil toward your right shoulder.

Sit up tall. Place both arms on the table. Keep your feet flat on the floor.

9

Students who have difficulty with the traditional pencil position may prefer the alternate method of holding the pencil between the first and second fingers.

### COACHING HINT

Right-handed teachers will better understand left-handed students if they practice the left-handed position themselves. The Zaner-Bloser Writing Frame can be used to show good hand position because the hand automatically settles into the correct position. Group left-handed writers together for instruction if you can do so without calling attention to the practice. They should be seated to the left of the chalkboard.

## FuN and GameS

### Left Hand, Right Hand, or Both?

Ask students to listen to the following directions and to pantomime the activities, using the hand you name.

*Pick up a pencil with your left hand.*
*Comb your hair with your right hand.*
*Catch a ball with both hands.*
*Write with your right hand.*
*Draw with your left hand.*
*Lift a box with both hands.*

(auditory, kinesthetic)

### Set the Table

Explain to students that knowing about left and right is important for more than just writing. Distribute large sheets of manila paper and crayons. Tell students that the paper represents a place mat and they will help set the table by drawing what is needed. Demonstrate at the chalkboard. Ask students to draw a plate in the center of the mat. Then ask them to draw a fork to the left of the plate and a knife and a spoon to the right of the plate. (visual, kinesthetic)

Check students' letter knowledge with an identification game. Ask them to point to letters on the page as you ask questions such as these:

Which lowercase letters are tall?
Which uppercase letters have slant lines?
Which uppercase letters look very different from their lowercase partner?
Which uppercase letters look similar to their lowercase partner?

Continue with questions about numerals.

*Practice Masters 62 and 63 are available for use with these pages.*

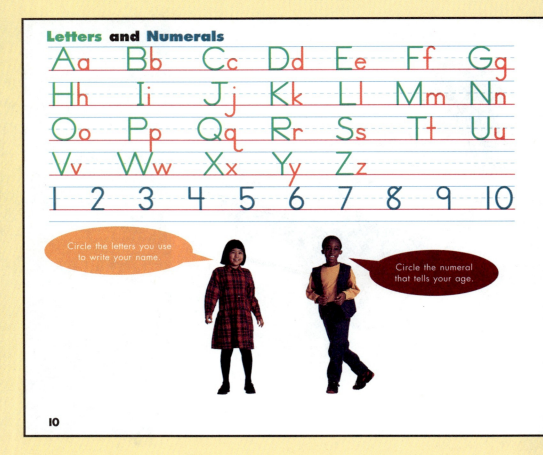

**Letters and Numerals**

Aa Bb Cc Dd Ee Ff Gg
Hh Ii Jj Kk Ll Mm Nn
Oo Pp Qq Rr Ss Tt Uu
Vv Ww Xx Yy Zz
1 2 3 4 5 6 7 8 9 10

Circle the letters you use to write your name.

Circle the numeral that tells your age.

10

Work through these pages with the students.

Guide students in locating and naming each guideline. Have them name its color and tell whether the line is solid or broken. Explain that using guidelines will help them write better letters.

Have students take turns naming the letters they use to write their names.

Review that tall letters touch both the headline and the baseline. Call attention to the fact that all the uppercase letters are tall. Ask students for other examples of tall letters.

To review short letters, explain that short letters touch the midline and the baseline. Ask students for examples of short letters.

Point out that some short letters like **g** go below the baseline and touch the headline of the next writing line. Ask students for examples of other short letters that go below the baseline.

Tall letters touch the headline.
All uppercase letters are tall.
Circle the tall letters.

b  c  d  D  v  F  h  m

Letters are tall or short.

Short letters touch the midline.
Circle the short letters.

a  c  f  i  P  n  o

Some letters go below the baseline.
Circle the letters that go below the baseline.

g  j  J  G  p  q  y  x  X

Write your name. Remember to begin with an uppercase letter.

Write the age you will be on your next birthday.

## EVALUATE

Invite students to compare the letters and numerals they wrote with the models they circled on the page.

To help students evaluate their writing, ask questions such as these:
Did you begin your name with an uppercase letter?
Does your uppercase letter begin at, or just below, the headline?
Does your uppercase letter rest on the baseline?
Did you use lowercase letters to write your name?
Does your numeral touch the headline and baseline?

Invite students to tell which letters they used and how the guidelines helped them.

## COACHING HINT

Refer students to these pages often as a guide for writing. Students will find them especially helpful when they write independently.

The development of self-evaluation skills is an important goal of handwriting instruction. It helps students become independent learners. By having students compare their letters with models, you have already begun this process. Be patient. Some students will be more able than others to evaluate their writing.

## FuN and GameS

**Letter Town, USA**
Invite students to make a set of tactile alphabet letter cards for a bulletin board display. Print each letter pair (uppercase and lowercase) on a blank index card and distribute the cards. Ask students to cover the letters with glue and then add glitter or small pieces of macaroni. Label the bulletin board *Letter Town, USA,* and invite students to visit and touch the letters often. (visual, kinesthetic)

**Tall or Short?**
Prepare a set of uppercase and lowercase alphabet letter cards and place them in a box. Include a set of numerals from 1 to 10. Write the headings *Tall* and *Short* on the chalkboard. Invite students to take turns selecting a card from the box and attaching it to the board under the correct heading. (visual)

## BEFORE WRITING

Tell students they will be looking for two kinds of straight lines on these pages.

One line stands up straight and is made with a pull down straight stroke. The other line lies down straight and is made with a slide right or slide left stroke.

## MODEL

Write pull down straight strokes on guidelines on the chalkboard. Model writing pull down straight strokes in the air and have students write in the air with you.

Follow the same procedure for slide right and slide left strokes.

**Pull Down Straight Lines**

Trace each pull down straight line.

L h I l i T n 5 g

Write these letters and numerals.

a B d t E 9 r H 4 F

Write these sentences.

I like to write.

This is my best writing.

Circle the letters with pull down straight lines.

12

**Pull Down Straight Lines**

Work through this page with the students.

First, ask students to look for the pull down straight lines in the letters and numerals. Have them trace each pull down straight line from top to bottom with a finger or the nonwriting end of a pencil.

Then help them complete the page.

## Slide Right and Slide Left Lines

Trace each slide right and slide left line.

L F H I G 7 t e 2

Write these letters and numerals.

e f t E 2 J H T G Z 5

Write these sentences.

September is a fall month.

Winter starts in December.

Circle the letters with slide right lines.

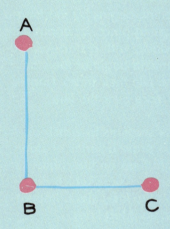

13

---

## Slide Right and Slide Left Lines

As you work through this page with the students, first ask them to look for slide right and slide left lines in the letters and numerals. Have them trace each slide right or slide left line with a finger or the non-writing end of a pencil.

Then help them complete the page.

## COACHING HINT

Have students name objects in the room formed with vertical lines. Explain that vertical lines are straight up and down. If possible, have students trace the lines with pull down straight strokes. (visual, kinesthetic)

### ABC Connect the Dots

Make a dot-to-dot series on the chalkboard and label each dot with an uppercase alphabet letter. Provide colored chalk for students to use. Choose volunteers to connect two labeled dots with either a pull down straight stroke or a slide right or slide left stroke as you give directions. (auditory, kinesthetic)

A

B          C

### Construct a Letter

Ask students to name the letters that are formed with only pull down straight and slide right or slide left strokes. List them (E, F, H, I, I, L, t, T) on the chalkboard. Cut construction paper into strips about one-half inch by three inches. Distribute strips and some glue. Demonstrate how to form a letter by gluing strips together. Tell students they will need to trim some strips. Have them make as many of the letters as time allows. (visual, kinesthetic)

Tell students they will be looking for circle lines and slant lines on these pages.

Draw two circles on the chalkboard. Show where a backward circle line begins by marking a starting place, at about one o'clock, with a star. Ask students to begin at the star and use their index fingers to trace over the line.

Show where a forward circle line begins by marking a starting place, at about nine o'clock, with a star. Ask students to begin at the star and use their index fingers to trace over the line.

Ask students to watch as you draw a series of slant right lines on the chalkboard. Ask in which direction the lines slant. Repeat for slant left lines.

## MODEL

Use your arms to model making backward circles (left) and forward circles (right) and have students copy you.

Write slant right and slant left strokes on guidelines on the chalkboard. Model writing the strokes in the air and have students write in the air with you.

## Circle Lines

Trace each circle line.

C 8 e a O b g d p

Write these letters and numerals.

o S s p 6 3 c D h Q

Write these sentences.

Pizza tastes good.

Peanut butter is better.

Circle the letters with circle lines.

14

## Circle Lines

Work through this page with the students.

First, ask students to look for the circle lines in the letters and numerals. Have them trace each circle line with a finger or the nonwriting end of a pencil.

Then help them complete the page.

## Slant Lines

Trace each slant line.

W Q A y X v w k 7

Write these letters and numerals.

w Y V K Z x M N y 7 2

Write these sentences.

My favorite color is green.

Blue and yellow make green.

Circle the letters with slant lines.

15

### Slant Lines

Work through this page with the students.

First, ask students to look for the slant lines in the letters and numerals. Have students trace each slant line with a finger or the nonwriting end of a pencil.

Then help them complete the page.

### COACHING HINT

Use an overhead projector to show pull down straight, slide right and slide left, circle, and slant lines. Ask students to wet their fingers in a cup of water and trace the enlarged lines on the chalkboard. (kinesthetic)

### Lines and Designs

Distribute drawing paper and crayons. Play some lively music and ask students to draw as they listen. Then stop the music. Have students share their drawings. As students show their work, ask classmates to identify lines that were formed with any of the basic strokes: pull down straight, slide right, slide left, circle backward, circle forward, slant left, slant right. (visual)

### Make and Shape Letters

Assign each student a letter pair (uppercase and lowercase) and distribute modeling clay. Have students form the letter pair with clay. When the letters are completed, assemble them on a table for a guessing game. Ask volunteers to close their eyes, trace a letter pair with a finger, and name the letter. (kinesthetic)

**Before You Go On . . . .**

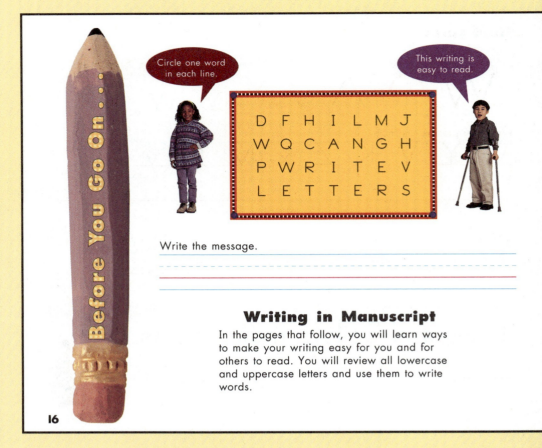

Circle one word in each line.

This writing is easy to read.

| D | F | H | I | L | M | J |
|---|---|---|---|---|---|---|
| W | Q | C | A | N | G | H |
| P | W | R | I | T | E | V |
| L | E | T | T | E | R | S |

Write the message.

### Writing in Manuscript

In the pages that follow, you will learn ways to make your writing easy for you and for others to read. You will review all lowercase and uppercase letters and use them to write words.

16

---

Use this page to introduce your students to the **Writing in Manuscript** section of the book. After students write the message from the word puzzle, discuss the content of this section.

## PREVIEW

Preview this section by calling attention to these features:

- letter models with numbered directional arrows
- guidelines for writing directly beneath handwriting models
- **My Own Words** writing space for familiar words
- opportunities for evaluating writing
- **On Your Own** activities with directions for independent writing

## PRACTICE MASTERS FOR WRITING IN MANUSCRIPT

- Letters, 1–52
- Numerals, 53
- Certificates, 55–57
- Letter to Parents—English, 58
- Letter to Parents—Spanish, 59
- Alphabet—English, 62
- Alphabet—Spanish, 63
- Stroke Descriptions—English, 64–67
- Stroke Descriptions—Spanish, 68–71
- Record of Student's Handwriting Skills, 54
- Zaner-Bloser Handwriting Grid, 94

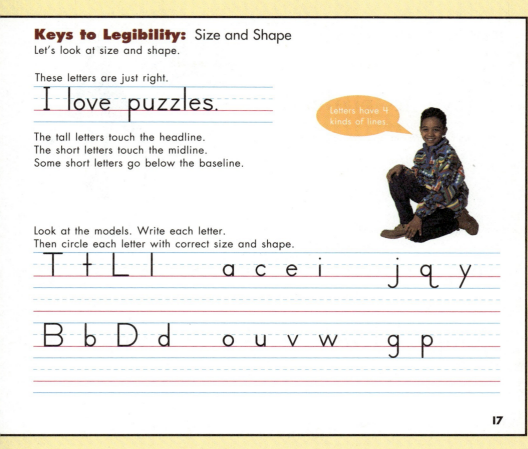

**Keys to Legibility:** Size and Shape

Let's look at size and shape.

These letters are just right.

I love puzzles.

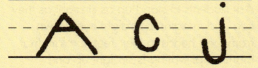

Letters have 4 kinds of lines.

The tall letters touch the headline.
The short letters touch the midline.
Some short letters go below the baseline.

Look at the models. Write each letter.
Then circle each letter with correct size and shape.

Tt Ll    a c e i    j q y

Bb Dd    o u v w    g p

17

---

The keys to legibility are introduced on pages 17, 18, and 19. You may wish to work through these pages with your students.

### MODEL THE WRITING

Write guidelines on the chalkboard. Have volunteers identify and name each guideline. Write an example of a tall letter, a short letter, and a letter that goes below the baseline. Ask students to name each letter and describe its size. Explain that writing letters the correct size and shape are two keys to making writing easy to read.

### EVALUATE

A c j

To help students evaluate the size and shape of their writing, ask questions such as these:
Do your tall letters touch the headline?
Do your short letters touch the midline?
Do letters that go below the baseline touch the next headline?
Are your letters easy to read?

### COACHING HINT

Prepare a set of cards with lowercase alphabet letters. Have a student or group of students sort the letters by size. Remind students that **g, j, p, q,** and **y** are short letters that go below the baseline. (visual)

## Keys to Legibility: Slant

Let's look at slant.

These letters are just right.

I love to pretend.

The letters are straight up and down.

Look at letters with pull down straight strokes.

Look at the models. Write each word.
Then circle each word in which the letters are straight up and down.

sing     act     dance     shout

jump     twirl     skip     clap

18

## MODEL THE WRITING

Ask students to stand up as straight as they can and imagine a straight line drawn from their heads to their feet. Explain that manuscript writing is straight up and down. Introduce the term *slant* to refer to this vertical quality. On guidelines on the chalkboard, write two words—one with letters that are straight up and down and one with letters that slant either left or right. Ask which example looks correct and have students explain why. Point out that writing letters straight up and down, with correct slant, is another key to making writing easy to read.

## EVALUATE

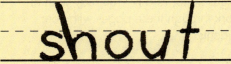

shout

To help students evaluate the slant of their letters, ask questions such as these:
Look at the word *shout*. Are the pull down straight strokes in **h, u,** and **t** straight up and down?
Look at the word *twirl*. Are the pull down straight strokes in **t, i, r,** and **l** straight up and down?

## COACHING HINT

You can evaluate the vertical quality of students' handwriting by drawing lines through the vertical strokes of the letters. If the lines are parallel, the vertical quality is correct.

## Keys to Legibility: Spacing

Let's look at spacing.

These words are just right.

I love jokes.

> Look at spaces between letters and between words.

The letters are not too close.
The letters are not too far apart.
There is a finger space between words.

Look at the models. Write each word.
Then circle each word with correct letter spacing.

silly    funny    cute    long

Put a star next to the sentence with good word spacing.
Then write the sentence correctly.

I know a joke.    I know a    joke.

## MODEL THE WRITING

On guidelines on the chalkboard, write *silly*, first with letters that are too close and then with letters that are too far apart. Ask students to explain what is wrong with the writing. Choose a volunteer to write the word with correct spacing. Add the word *jokes*, placing a finger between the words. Explain that writing with correct spacing between letters in a word, and between words, is another key to making writing easy to read.

## EVALUATE

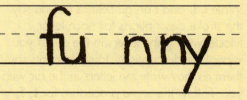

fu nny

To help students evaluate the spacing in their writing, ask questions such as these: Look at the word *funny*. Are the letters in the word too close or too far apart? Is there room for a finger space between the words *a* and *joke* in your sentence? Is your sentence easy to read?

## COACHING HINT

Review the keys to legibility—size and shape, slant, and spacing. Provide colored chalk for students to use at the chalkboard. Have them take turns correcting and rewriting words with incorrect size and shape, slant, or spacing. (visual, kinesthetic)

## CONTINUOUS STROKE

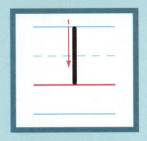

Touch the headline; pull down straight to the baseline.

Touch the midline; pull down straight to the baseline. Lift. Dot.

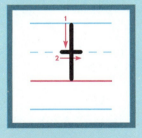

Touch the headline; pull down straight to the base-line. Lift. Touch the midline; slide right.

## FuN and GameS

### Guess Who?
Have the students write their names on the chalkboard. Ask them to look for names that have l, i, or t. Play a guessing game with the names, for example: *I am thinking of a girl. Her name begins with L. There are two t's in her name. Who is she?* (auditory, visual, kinesthetic)

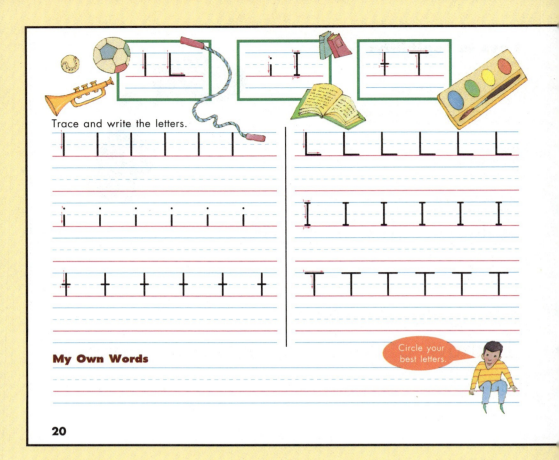

Trace and write the letters.

**My Own Words**

Circle your best letters.

20

## Model the Writing
Write l, i, and t on guidelines as you say the stroke descriptions for each letter. Model writing the letters in the air as you repeat the descriptions. Have students say them as they write the letters in the air with you. Follow the same procedure for L, I, and T.

## A Closer Look
Call attention to the size and shape of the letters by asking questions such as these:
Which letters are tall?
Which letter is short?
Which stroke begins each letter?
Which letters have a slide right stroke?

## Practice
Let students practice writing the letter pairs lL, iI, and tT on laminated writing cards or slates before they write on the pages.

Note: In each Evaluate section, the letter-forms illustrate common problems in letter formation.

## Evaluate

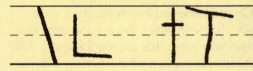

To help students evaluate their writing, ask questions such as these:
Is your l straight up and down?
Does your L begin at the headline?
Does your i begin at the midline?
Is your I about the same width as the model?
Is the slide right stroke of your t on the midline?
Are the strokes in your T straight?

## Better Letters

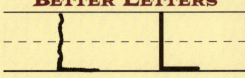

To help students write pull down straight strokes correctly, remind them to pull, not draw, the strokes.

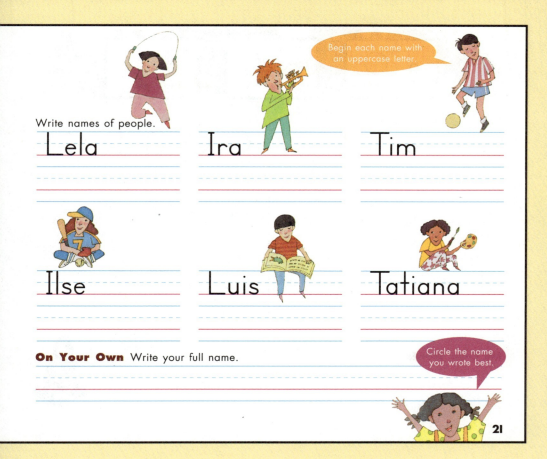

Write names of people.

Begin each name with an uppercase letter.

Lela

Ira

Tim

Ilse

Luis

Tatiana

**On Your Own** Write your full name.

Circle the name you wrote best.

21

## WRITE LEGIBLY

Before students write, call attention to the size and shape of letters. Point out that names begin with uppercase letters and all uppercase letters are tall.

After they write, have them compare their letters with the models. Guide students to recognize why one name they wrote might be better than another.

## COACHING HINT

To accommodate the needs of students with various modality strengths, introduce letters in three steps:
1. Talk about the letter—its size, shape, and strokes. (auditory)
2. Demonstrate the letter on the chalkboard. (visual)
3. Have students trace the letter in the air or on some other surface. (kinesthetic)

## PRACTICE MASTERS 1–6

Trace and write.

line    little    lived    lion    let

liked    look    late    letter    land

Write your own words.

Name

Copyright © Zaner-Bloser, Inc.

Trace and write.

L L L L L L L L

Luisa and I write lots of lists.

Larry writes very long letters.

Trace and write.

i i i i i i i i i i

is    it    if    in    ill    invite

inch    ice    into    inside    isn't

Write your own words.

Name

Copyright © Zaner-Bloser, Inc.

Trace and write.

I I I I I I I I

Ida likes the winter season best.

Ira always likes the spring.

Trace and write.

t t t t t t t t

two    too    tall    talk    ten    three

this    thing    then    take    told

Write your own words.

Name

Copyright © Zaner-Bloser, Inc.

Trace and write.

T T T T T T T T

Tere has the first turn at bat.

Tama's turn is after Tere's.

Write about a game you play.

Name

Copyright © Zaner-Bloser, Inc.

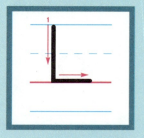
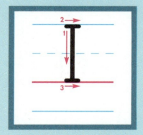

## CONTINUOUS STROKE

Touch the headline; pull down straight to the baseline. Slide right.

Touch the headline; pull down straight to the baseline. Lift. Touch the headline; slide right. Lift. Touch the baseline; slide right.

Touch the headline; pull down straight to the baseline. Lift. Touch the headline; slide right.

## Write Away

**Lucy Likes Lemonade**
Invite students to say these alliterative sentences with you.

Lucy likes lemonade.
Ida is in Ireland.
Todd tied ten ties.

Ask students to write other alliterative sentences about Lucy, Ida, and Todd. (auditory)

## CONTINUOUS STROKE

Touch below the midline; circle back (left) all the way around.

Touch below the midline; circle back (left) all the way around. Push up straight to the midline. Pull down straight to the baseline.

Touch below the midline; circle back (left) all the way around. Push up straight to the headline. Pull down straight to the baseline.

## FuN and Games

**O, My Name Is . . .**
Write this pattern on the chalkboard:

O, my name is (Olive).
I live in (Oklahoma),
and I like (ostriches).

Repeat the pattern with students, using **aA** and **dD**. (auditory, visual)

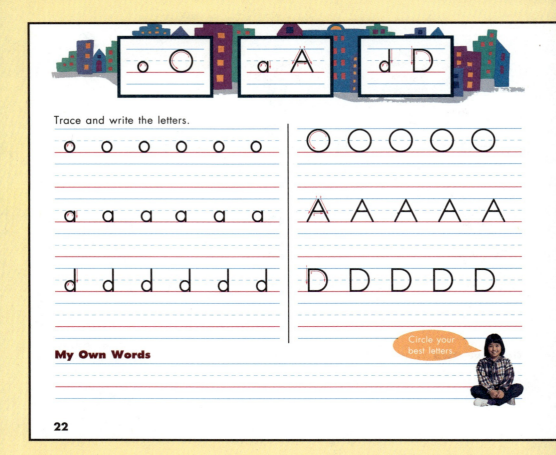

Trace and write the letters.

o o o o o o     O O O O O

a a a a a a     A A A A A

d d d d d d     D D D D D

**My Own Words**

Circle your best letters.

## MODEL THE WRITING

Write **o**, **a**, and **d** on guidelines as you say the stroke descriptions for each letter. Have students use their fingers to trace the models **o**, **a**, and **d** in their books as you repeat the descriptions. Follow the same procedure for **O**, **A**, and **D**.

## A CLOSER LOOK

Call attention to the size and shape of the letters by asking questions such as these:
Which letters are tall?
Which letters are short?
Which letters look alike except for their size?
Which letters begin with a backward circle stroke?
Which letters have slide right strokes?
Which letter has two slant strokes?

## PRACTICE

Let students practice writing the letter pairs **oO**, **aA**, and **dD** on laminated writing cards or slates before they write on the pages.

## EVALUATE

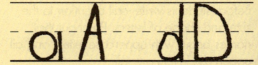

To help students evaluate their writing, ask questions such as these:
Are your **o** and **O** round?
Does your pull down straight stroke in **a** touch the circle?
Is your **A** about the same width as the model?
Is the backward circle in your **d** round?
Is your **D** about the same width as the model?

## BETTER LETTERS

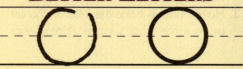

To help students make backward circle strokes correctly, remind them to close the circle properly.

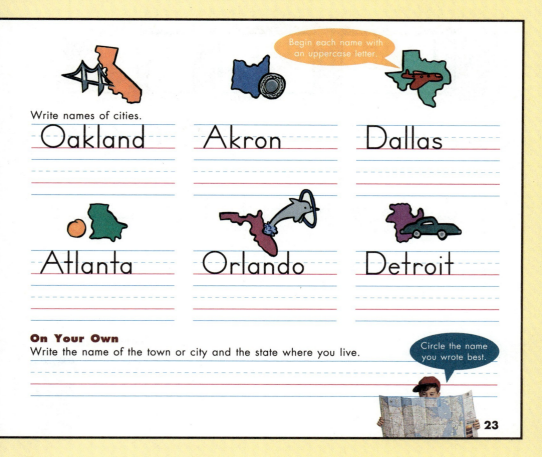

Write names of cities.

Begin each name with an uppercase letter.

Oakland  Akron  Dallas

Atlanta  Orlando  Detroit

**On Your Own**
Write the name of the town or city and the state where you live.

Circle the name you wrote best.

23

## WRITE LEGIBLY

Before students write, call attention to the spacing between letters in one of the names on the page. Help students conclude that none of the letters in the word touch.

After they write, have students compare their spacing of letters in words with the models. Guide students to recognize why one name they wrote might be better than another.

## COACHING HINT

To help students understand the term *below*, make widely spaced guidelines on the floor with masking tape. Identify each guideline and label it. Then give directions for students to stand below the guideline you name. Invite students to "walk" the letters **o, O, a,** and **d** as you say the stroke descriptions. (auditory, kinesthetic)

## PRACTICE MASTERS 7–12

## CONTINUOUS STROKE

Touch below the headline; circle back (left) all the way around.

Touch the headline; slant left to the baseline. Lift. Touch the headline; slant right to the baseline. Lift. Touch the midline; slide right.

Touch the headline; pull down straight to the baseline. Lift. Touch the headline; slide right; curve forward (right) to the baseline; slide left.

## Write Away

**Away We Go!**
Invite students to make a poster showing a favorite place in their town or city or a place they have visited. Then have them label the poster and add a caption, such as *Come Visit Us!* (visual)

## CONTINUOUS STROKE

Touch below the midline; circle back (left), ending above the baseline.

Touch halfway between the midline and baseline; slide right; circle back (left), ending above the baseline.

Touch below the headline; curve back (left); pull down straight to the baseline. Lift. Touch the midline; slide right.

### FuN and Games

**Cats, Elephants, and Foxes**

Invite students to draw a cat, an elephant, or a fox. Distribute writing paper and ask students to write words that begin with the same letter as the animal name. (visual, auditory, kinesthetic)

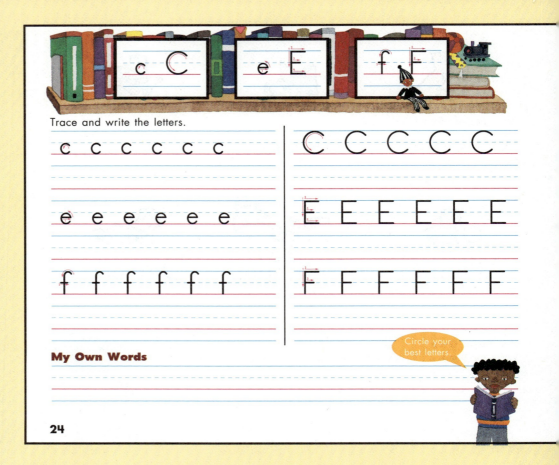

Trace and write the letters.

c c c c c c    C C C C C

e e e e e e    E E E E E

f f f f f f    F F F F F

**My Own Words**

Circle your best letters.

## MODEL THE WRITING

Write **c**, **e**, and **f** on guidelines as you say the stroke descriptions. Invite students to use their index fingers to write these letters on their desks as you repeat the descriptions and they say them with you. Follow the same procedure for **C**, **E**, and **F**.

## A CLOSER LOOK

Call attention to the size and shape of the letters by asking questions such as these:
Which letters are short?
Which letters are tall?
Which letters begin with a backward circle stroke?
Which letters begin with a pull down straight stroke?
Which letters look alike except for their size?

## PRACTICE

Let students practice writing the letter pairs **cC**, **eE**, and **fF** on laminated writing cards or slates before they write on the pages.

## EVALUATE

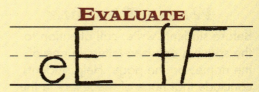

To help students evaluate their writing, ask questions such as these:
Do your **c** and **C** look like a circle that has not been closed?
Does your slide right stroke in **e** touch your circle back stroke?
Are the top and bottom slide right strokes in your **E** the same width?
Does your **f** begin below the headline?
Is your **F** straight up and down?

## BETTER LETTERS

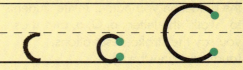

To help students write **c** and **C** correctly, place dots for the beginning and ending points of the letters.

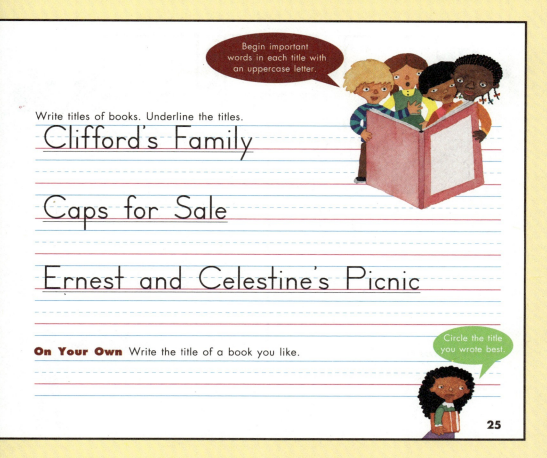

Begin important words in each title with an uppercase letter.

Write titles of books. Underline the titles.

Clifford's Family

Caps for Sale

Ernest and Celestine's Picnic

**On Your Own** Write the title of a book you like.

Circle the title you wrote best.

25

## WRITE LEGIBLY

Before students write, call attention to the spacing between words in the titles of the books. Remind students that the space shows where one word ends and another begins.

After they write, have students compare their spacing between words with the spacing in the models. Guide them to recognize why one title they wrote might be better than another.

## COACHING HINT

Encourage students to write with vertical slant. If students write letters that are not vertical, check to see if they need practice with any of the following: positioning the paper correctly, pulling the downstrokes in the proper direction, shifting the paper as the writing line fills.

**PRACTICE MASTERS 13–18**

Touch below the headline; circle back (left), ending above the baseline.

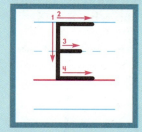

Touch the headline; pull down straight to the baseline. Lift. Touch the headline; slide right. Lift. Touch the midline; slide right. Stop short. Lift. Touch the baseline; slide right.

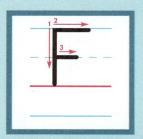

Touch the headline; pull down straight to the baseline. Lift. Touch the headline; slide right. Lift. Touch the midline; slide right. Stop short.

## Write Away

**Make Bookmarks**
Invite students to make bookmarks about books they like. Have them write the book title and draw a picture to decorate an oak tag strip. (visual, kinesthetic)

Touch below the midline; circle back (left) all the way around. Push up straight to the midline. Pull down straight through the baseline; curve back (left).

Touch the midline; pull down straight through the baseline; curve back (left). Lift. Dot.

Touch below the midline; circle back (left) all the way around. Push up straight to the midline. Pull down straight through the baseline; curve forward (right).

## Fun and Games

### Charades

Write a noun that begins with **g**, **j**, or **q** on each of twelve index cards. Have each student choose a word and act it out until a classmate guesses it and writes it on the board. (visual)

**26**

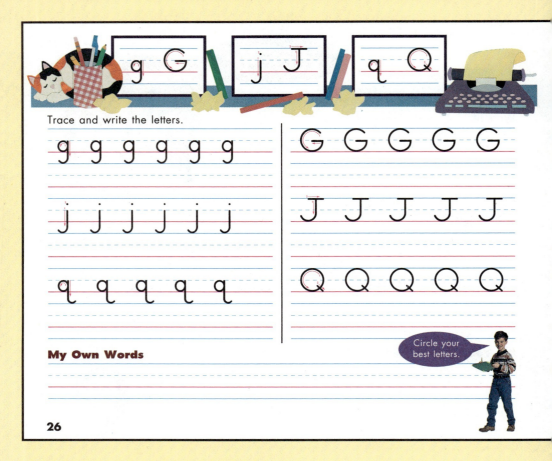

Trace and write the letters.

g g g g g g     G G G G G

j j j j j j     J J J J J

q q q q q q     Q Q Q Q Q

**My Own Words**

Circle your best letters.

26

## Model the Writing

Write **g**, **j**, and **q** on guidelines as you say the stroke descriptions for each letter. Invite several students to dip a small sponge in water and use it to write these letters on the chalkboard while others say the descriptions with you. Follow the same procedure for **G**, **J**, and **Q**.

## A Closer Look

Call attention to the size and shape of the letters by asking questions such as these:
Which letters are tall?
Which letters go below the baseline?
Which letters have a backward circle?
Which letters begin with a pull down straight stroke?
Which letter has a slide left stroke?

## Practice

Let students practice writing the letter pairs **gG**, **jJ**, and **qQ** on laminated writing cards or slates before they write on the pages.

## Evaluate

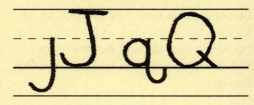

To help students evaluate their writing, ask questions such as these:
Is the backward circle of your **g** round?
Does the slide left stroke of your **G** touch the midline?
Did you remember to dot your **j**?
Is your **J** straight up and down?
Does your **q** touch the next headline?
Does your **Q** look like an **O** except for the slant right stroke?

## Better Letters

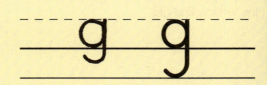

Remind students that descenders should fill the space below the baseline and touch the next headline.

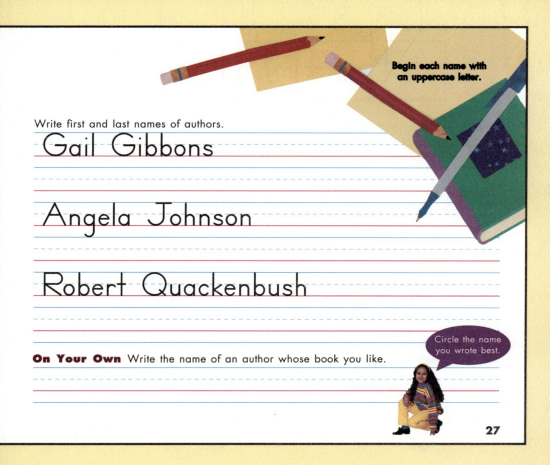

Write first and last names of authors.

Gail Gibbons

Angela Johnson

Robert Quackenbush

Begin each name with an uppercase letter.

**On Your Own** Write the name of an author whose book you like.

Circle the name you wrote best.

27

## WRITE LEGIBLY

Before students write, call attention to the position of letters on the guidelines. Point out that **g, j,** and **q** are examples of short letters that go below the baseline and touch the next headline.

After they write, have students compare their letters with the models. Guide them to recognize why one name might be written better than another.

## COACHING HINT

Write **g, j,** and **q** on guidelines on the chalkboard. Focus on the part of the letter that descends below the baseline. Have students trace over that part of each letter with colored chalk. Point out where the curve of each letter begins and ends. Explain that it rests on the headline of the next writing space. For further reinforcement, have students make **g, j,** and **q** from pipe cleaners or play dough. (visual, kinesthetic)

## PRACTICE MASTERS 19–24

Touch below the headline; circle back (left), ending at the midline. Slide left.

Touch the headline; pull down straight; curve back (left). Lift. Touch the headline; slide right.

Touch below the headline; circle back (left) all the way around. Lift. Slant right to the baseline.

## Write Away

**Design a Book Jacket** Have students choose a familiar book and make a book jacket for it. Distribute drawing paper and markers. Ask that they include the title of the book, the author's name, and an illustration on the front cover. On the back, have them write about the book. (visual, kinesthetic)

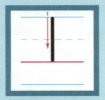

Touch the headline; pull down straight to the baseline.

Touch below the headline; curve forward (right); slant left to the baseline. Slide right.

Touch below the headline; curve forward (right) to the midline; curve forward (right), ending above the baseline.

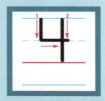

Touch the headline; pull down straight to the midline. Slide right. Lift. Move to the right and touch the headline; pull down straight to the baseline.

Touch the headline; pull down straight to the midline. Circle forward (right), ending above the baseline. Lift. Touch the headline; slide right.

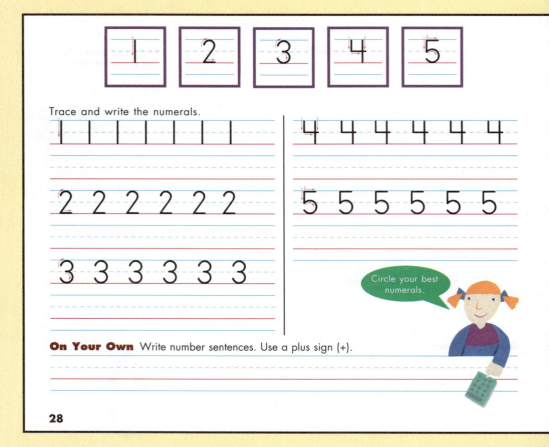

Trace and write the numerals.

Circle your best numerals.

**On Your Own** Write number sentences. Use a plus sign (+).

28

## MODEL THE WRITING

Write 1, 2, 3, 4, and 5 on guidelines as you say the stroke descriptions for each numeral. Model writing the numerals in the air as you repeat the descriptions. Have students say them as they write the letters in the air with you. Follow the same procedure with 6, 7, 8, 9, and 10.

## A CLOSER LOOK

Call attention to the size and shape of the numerals by asking questions such as these:
Do all these numerals touch the headline and baseline?
Which numerals have only straight lines?
Which numerals have slide right strokes?
Which numeral has two curve forward strokes?
Which numerals have a slant stroke?

## PRACTICE

Let students practice writing the numerals 1, 2, 3, 4, 5, 6, 7, 8, 9, and 10 on laminated writing cards or slates before they write on the page.

## EVALUATE

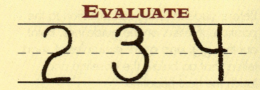

To help students evaluate their writing, ask questions such as these:
Is the pull down stroke in your 1 straight?
Is the slant left stroke in your 2 straight?
Are both parts of your 3 the same size?
Are the strokes in your 4 straight?
Does your 5 rest on the baseline?

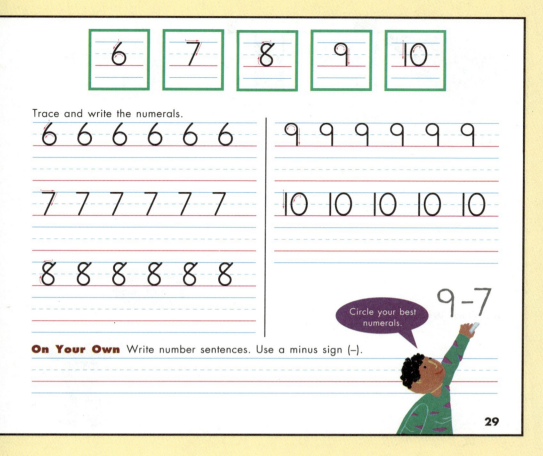

Trace and write the numerals.

6 6 6 6 6 6

9 9 9 9 9 9

7 7 7 7 7 7

10 10 10 10 10

8 8 8 8 8 8

9-7

Circle your best numerals.

**On Your Own** Write number sentences. Use a minus sign (–).

29

---

## EVALUATE

To help students evaluate their writing, ask questions such as these:

Does your **6** begin at the headline with a curve down stroke?

Are both strokes of your **7** straight?

Are the curves of your **8** about the same size?

Does your **9** have a round backward circle?

Is there a space between **1** and **0** in your **10**?

## COACHING HINT

Emphasize the importance of legible numeral formation whenever students write numerals. Discuss problems that can arise if numerals are not formed correctly. (visual, auditory)

**PRACTICE MASTER 53**

Trace and write.
1 2 3 4 5    8 + 2 = 10
6 7 8 9 10   9 – 8 = 1

Write some number sentences. Use + and –

Name

Copyright © Zaner-Bloser, Inc.        PRACTICE MASTER 53

---

Touch the headline; curve down to the baseline; curve up to the midline and around to close the circle.

Touch the headline; slide right. Slant left to the baseline.

Touch below the headline; curve back (left); curve forward (right), touching the baseline; slant up (right) to the headline.

Touch below the headline; circle back (left) all the way around. Pull down straight to the baseline.

Touch the headline; pull down straight to the baseline. Lift. Touch the headline; curve down to the baseline; curve up to the headline.

## CONTINUOUS STROKE

Touch the midline; pull down straight; curve forward (right); push up to the midline. Pull down straight to the baseline.

Touch below the midline; curve back (left); curve forward (right), ending above the baseline.

## FᵁN and Games

**Under the Umbrella**
Draw a large umbrella and a winding snake on the chalkboard, or cut them from construction paper. Place the snake under the umbrella. Ask students to write words that begin with **u** or **s** on colorful squares of paper with guidelines and place them under the umbrella. (visual, kinesthetic)

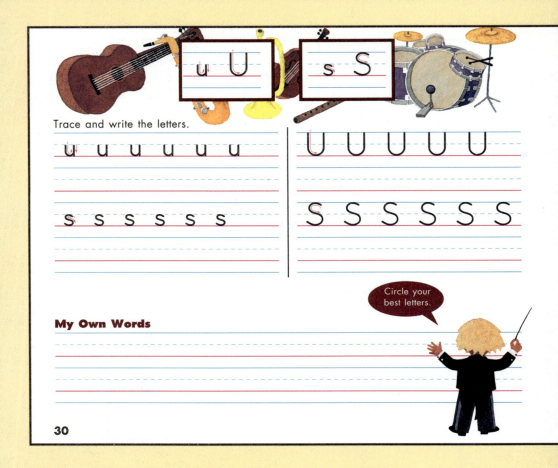

Trace and write the letters.

U U U U U U     U U U U U

s s s s s s     S S S S S

**My Own Words**

Circle your best letters.

30

## MODEL THE WRITING

Write **u** and **s** on guidelines as you say the stroke descriptions for each letter. Have students use their fingers to trace the models in their books as you repeat the descriptions. Follow the same procedure for **U** and **S**.

## A CLOSER LOOK

Call attention to the size and shape of the letters by asking questions such as these:
Which letters are short?
Which letters have curve backward and curve forward strokes?
How are **s** and **S** different?
Which letter ends on the baseline?
Which letter ends at the headline?

## PRACTICE

Let students practice writing the letter pairs **uU** and **sS** on laminated writing cards or slates before they write on the pages.

## EVALUATE

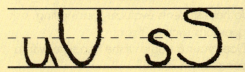

To help students evaluate their writing, ask questions such as these:
Are the pull down straight strokes in your **u** straight?
Does the curve of your **U** begin and end halfway between the midline and baseline?
Does your **s** begin just below the midline?
Is the top of your **S** about the same size as the bottom?

## BETTER LETTERS

To help students make **s** (or **S**) correctly, make two circles, one on top of the other, then outline the curves.

## CONTINUOUS STROKE

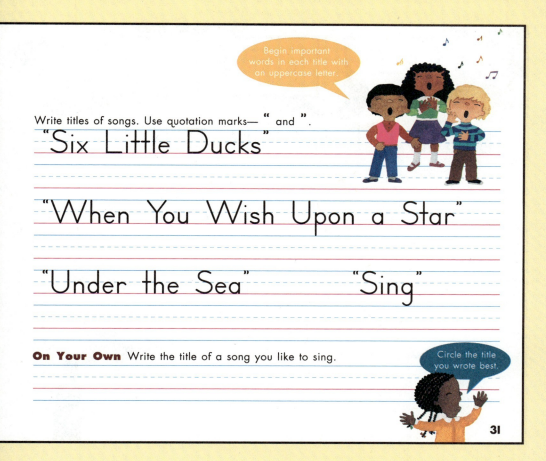

Write titles of songs. Use quotation marks— " and ".

"Six Little Ducks"

"When You Wish Upon a Star"

"Under the Sea"　　　　"Sing"

**On Your Own** Write the title of a song you like to sing.

*Begin important words in each title with an uppercase letter.*

*Circle the title you wrote best.*

31

Touch the headline; pull down straight; curve forward (right); push up to the headline.

Touch below the headline; curve back (left); curve forward (right), ending above the baseline.

## WRITE LEGIBLY

Before students write, call attention to the size and shape of tall letters. Point out that tall letters are written between the headline and baseline and that all uppercase letters are tall.

After they write, have them compare the size of their letters to the models. Guide students to see why one title they wrote might be written better than another.

## COACHING HINT

Making sandpaper letters and having students trace them as you say the stroke descriptions will be helpful to students who have problems with small-muscle coordination and difficulty in writing letters. Guide students' fingers as they trace the letters uU and sS in one continuous motion. Forming letters in a tray of smooth wet sand is another good way to practice continuous strokes. (kinesthetic)

## PRACTICE MASTERS 25–28

## Write Away

**Sing! Sing! Sing!** Brainstorm names of familiar children's songs. Then ask students to write two of their favorites on handwriting paper. Collect the papers, and write the lyrics to the songs on chart paper so students can follow along as they sing. Sing a few songs each day until all their favorites have been sung. (auditory, visual)

31

## CONTINUOUS STROKE

Touch the headline; pull down straight to the baseline. Push up; circle forward (right) all the way around.

Touch the midline; pull down straight through the baseline to the next guideline. Push up; circle forward (right) all the way around.

Touch the midline; pull down straight to the baseline. Push up; curve forward (right).

## FᵁN and GameS

**Guess What?**
Ask *What has long floppy ears and hops?* Choose a student to write the answer on the board. Point out that the answer begins with **r** (rabbit) or **b** (bunny). Then have students take turns asking one-sentence riddle questions. (auditory, kinesthetic)

32

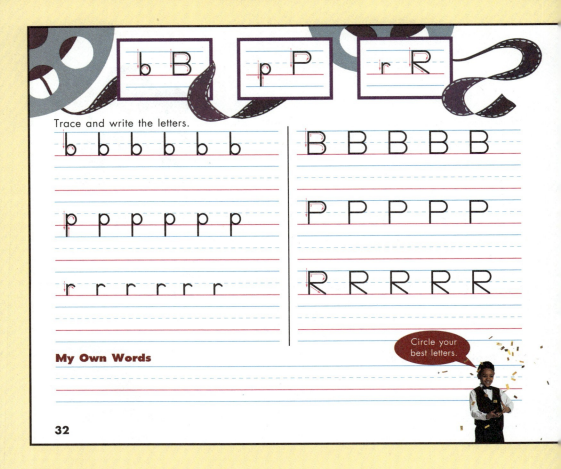

Trace and write the letters.

b b b b b b     B B B B B

p p p p p     P P P P

r r r r r r     R R R R R

**My Own Words**

Circle your best letters.

32

## MODEL THE WRITING

Write **b**, **p**, and **r** on guidelines as you say the stroke descriptions for each letter. Invite students to use their index fingers to trace the letters on sandpaper as they repeat the descriptions with you. Follow the same procedure for **B**, **P**, and **R**.

## A CLOSER LOOK

Call attention to the size and shape of the letters by asking questions such as these:
Which stroke is used to begin all the letters?
Which letter goes below the baseline?
Which letters have a push up stroke that retraces the pull down stroke?
Which letter has a slant stroke?
Which letters have slide left strokes?

## PRACTICE

Let students practice writing the letter pairs **bB**, **pP**, and **rR** on laminated writing cards or slates before they write on the pages.

## EVALUATE

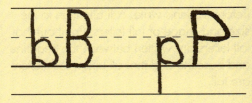

To help students evaluate their writing, ask questions such as these:
Does your **b** have a round forward circle?
Is your **B** about the same width as the model?
Is your forward circle in **p** round?
Are the slide right and slide left strokes in your **P** the same width?
Did you retrace carefully in your **r**?
Is your **R** straight up and down?

## BETTER LETTERS

Remind students to push up (retrace) carefully to avoid making a loop when writing **r** and other letters with retraces.

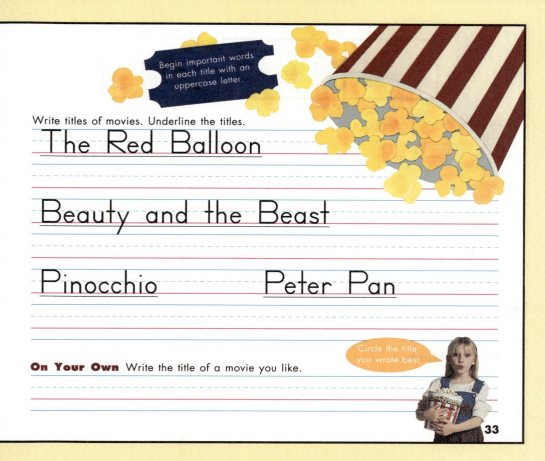

Begin important words in each title with an uppercase letter.

Write titles of movies. Underline the titles.

The Red Balloon

Beauty and the Beast

Pinocchio          Peter Pan

**On Your Own** Write the title of a movie you like.

Circle the title you wrote best.

33

## WRITE LEGIBLY

Before students write, call attention to the slant of the letters. Remind students that manuscript letters are written straight up and down. Demonstrate by writing **b** once in correct vertical position and once slanting left. Ask a volunteer to circle the correct one.

After students write, have them compare their letters with the models to see if their letters are straight up and down. Guide students to recognize why one title they wrote might be written better than another.

## COACHING HINT

To help avoid confusion about when to use a backward circle or a forward circle, explain that if a circle in a letter comes before the vertical stroke, it is always a backward circle, as in **a, d, g,** and **q.** If a vertical stroke in a letter comes before the circle, the circle is always a forward circle, as in **b** and **p.** (visual)

**PRACTICE MASTERS 29–34**

Trace and write.
b b b b b b b b
bat best birds brother buy
both book before bus bug
Write your own words.
Name
Copyright © Zaner-Bloser, Inc.

Trace and write.
B B B B B B B B
Bene has a brown book bag.
Binh's book bag is bright blue.

Trace and write.
P P P P P P P P
pet putting plant pull pot
paper paid play people pass
Write your own words.
Name
Copyright © Zaner-Bloser, Inc.

Trace and write.
P P P P P P P P
Peg made a paper puzzle.
Paki made a paper airplane.

Trace and write.
r r r r r r r r
rain read rest roar rose
race reach riding real rug
Write your own words.
Name
Copyright © Zaner-Bloser, Inc.

Trace and write.
R R R R R R R R
Rita is wearing a red raincoat.
Reed is wearing a green shirt.
Write about something you are wearing today.
Name
Copyright © Zaner-Bloser, Inc.

## CONTINUOUS STROKE

Touch the headline; pull down straight to the baseline. Lift. Touch the headline; slide right; curve forward (right) to the midline; slide left. Slide right; curve forward (right) to the baseline; slide left.

Touch the headline; pull down straight to the baseline. Lift. Touch the headline; slide right; curve forward (right) to the midline; slide left.

Touch the headline; pull down straight to the baseline. Lift. Touch the headline; slide right; curve forward (right) to the midline; slide left. Slant right to the baseline.

## Write Away

Invite children to make up a title for a new movie. Ask them to write a list of characters for the movie. (kinesthetic)

33

## CONTINUOUS STROKE

Touch the midline; pull down straight to the baseline. Push up; curve forward (right); pull down straight to the baseline.

Touch the midline; pull down straight to the baseline. Push up; curve forward (right); pull down straight to the baseline. Push up; curve forward (right); pull down straight to the baseline.

Touch the headline; pull down straight to the baseline. Push up; curve forward (right); pull down straight to the baseline.

## FᵘN and GameS

### Sense or Nonsense?

Write a story on the chalkboard with fill-in blanks. Ask students to write words or phrases that begin with **n**, **m**, or **h**. (visual)

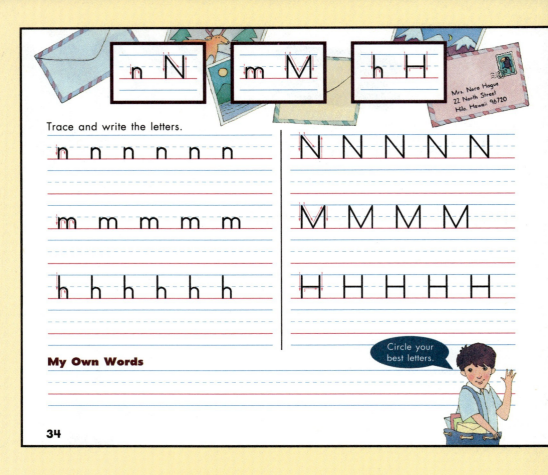

Trace and write the letters.

My Own Words

Circle your best letters.

34

## MODEL THE WRITING

Write **n**, **m**, and **h** on guidelines as you say the stroke descriptions for each letter. Invite several students to dip small sponges in water and to use them to write these letters on the chalkboard while others say the descriptions with you. Follow the same procedure for **N**, **M**, and **H**.

## A CLOSER LOOK

Call attention to the size and shape of the letters by asking questions such as these:
Which stroke begins **N**, **M**, and **H**?
Which letters have slant right strokes?
Which letter has a slide right line?
Which lowercase letter is a tall letter?
Which letters have a curve forward stroke?

## PRACTICE

Let students practice writing the letter pairs **nN**, **mM**, and **hH** on laminated writing cards or slates before they write on the pages.

## EVALUATE

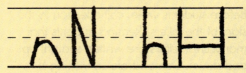

To help students evaluate their writing, ask questions such as these:
Are the pull down straight strokes in your **n** straight?
Is your **N** about the same width as the model?
Does the curve forward stroke of your **h** touch the midline?
Does the slide right stroke of your **H** touch the midline?

## BETTER LETTERS

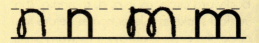

Remind students to push up (retrace) carefully to avoid making loops when writing **n** and **m**.

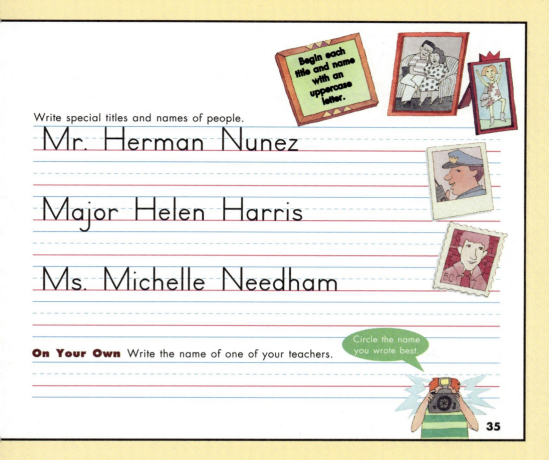

Write special titles and names of people.

Begin each title and name with an uppercase letter.

# Mr. Herman Nunez

# Major Helen Harris

# Ms. Michelle Needham

**On Your Own** Write the name of one of your teachers.

Circle the name you wrote best.

35

## WRITE LEGIBLY

Before students write, call attention to the end marks that follow special titles used with people's names. Have the titles with end marks read aloud.

After students write, have them compare their writing with the models. Guide students to recognize why one name might be written better than another.

## COACHING HINT

You can help evaluate the vertical quality of students' handwriting by drawing lines through the vertical strokes of their letters. If the lines are parallel, the vertical quality is correct. (visual)

## PRACTICE MASTERS 35–40

Touch the headline; pull down straight to the baseline. Lift. Touch the headline; slant right to the baseline. Push up straight to the headline.

Touch the headline; pull down straight to the baseline. Lift. Touch the headline; slant right to the baseline. Slant up (right) to the headline. Pull down straight to the baseline.

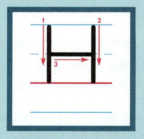

Touch the headline; pull down straight to the baseline. Lift. Move to the right and touch the headline; pull down straight to the baseline. Lift. Move to the left and touch the midline; slide right.

## Write Away

**Just a Note**
Have children write a note to an adult, using the person's title. (kinesthetic)

## CONTINUOUS STROKE

Touch the midline; slant right to the baseline. Slant up (right) to the midline.

Touch the midline; slant right to the baseline. Lift. Move to the right and touch the midline; slant left through the baseline.

Touch the midline; slant right to the baseline. Slant up (right) to the midline. Slant right to the baseline. Slant up (right) to the midline.

## FuN and Games

### Letters in Color

Have students practice writing v, y, w, and other letters using paints and cotton swabs. Ask them to form letters as you say the stroke descriptions. Then have students say the stroke descriptions as classmates write the letters. (auditory, kinesthetic)

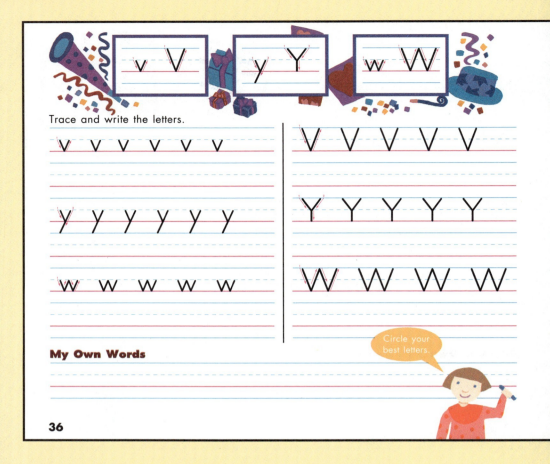

Trace and write the letters.

**My Own Words**

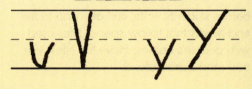

Circle your best letters.

## MODEL THE WRITING

Write v, y, and w on guidelines as you say the stroke descriptions for each letter. Model writing the letters in the air as you repeat the descriptions. Have students say them as they write the letters in the air with you. Follow the same procedure for V, Y, and W.

## A CLOSER LOOK

Call attention to the size and shape of the letters by asking questions such as these:
Which stroke is used in all these letters?
Which letters look the same except for their size?
Which letters are short?
Which letter goes below the baseline?
Where do you start writing all these uppercase letters?

## PRACTICE

Let students practice writing the letter pairs vV, yY, and wW on laminated writing cards or slates before they write on the pages.

## EVALUATE

To help students evaluate their writing, ask questions such as these:
Are your slant strokes in v straight?
Is your V about the same width as the model?
Does your y touch the headline of the next space?
Does your Y end with a pull down straight stroke?
Are the slant strokes in your w straight?
Does your W begin at the headline?

## BETTER LETTERS

Stress that all the strokes slant right.

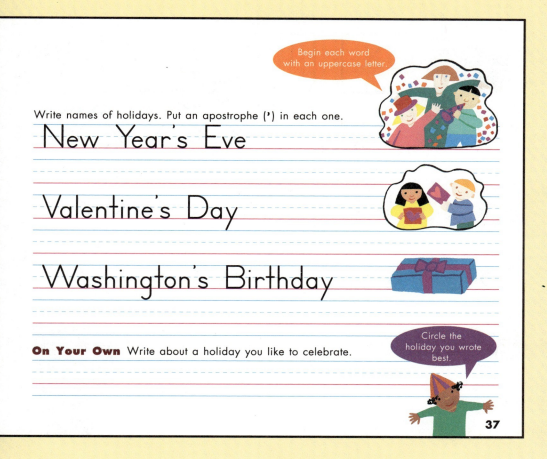

Write names of holidays. Put an apostrophe (') in each one.

*Begin each word with an uppercase letter.*

New Year's Eve

Valentine's Day

Washington's Birthday

**On Your Own** Write about a holiday you like to celebrate.

*Circle the holiday you wrote best.*

37

## WRITE LEGIBLY

Before students write, call attention to the spacing between words. Remind students to leave a finger space between words. After students write, have them compare their writing with the models. Guide students to recognize why the spacing in one holiday name might be better than the spacing in another.

## COACHING HINT

If students have not mastered a handwriting skill or stroke, provide additional instruction and practice. Reinforce instruction with activities geared to each student's modality strengths. Help them evaluate their writing.

## PRACTICE MASTERS 41–46

Touch the headline; slant right to the baseline. Slant up (right) to the headline.

Touch the headline; slant right to the midline. Lift. Move to the right and touch the headline; slant left to the midline. Pull down straight to the baseline.

Touch the headline; slant right to the baseline. Slant up (right) to the headline. Slant right to the baseline. Slant up (right) to the headline.

## Write Away

**Which Holiday Is It?** Invite students to name holidays they know. List them on the chalkboard. Have students choose one and write a description of an activity or an item they associate with the holiday. (visual, kinesthetic)

## CONTINUOUS STROKE

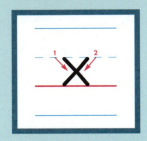

Touch the midline; slant right to the baseline. Lift. Move to the right and touch the midline; slant left to the baseline.

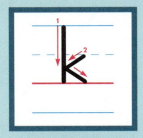

Touch the headline; pull down straight to the baseline. Lift. Move to the right and touch the midline; slant left. Slant right to the baseline.

Touch the midline; slide right. Slant left to the baseline. Slide right.

## FᵘN and Games

### Listen and Write

On the chalkboard, write the spelling patterns -ack, -ox, and -zz. Give clues like those below and ask a student to write each answer under the correct pattern. *A boy's name ending in -ack. An animal ending in -ox. A sound a bee makes ending in -zz.* (visual, auditory, kinesthetic)

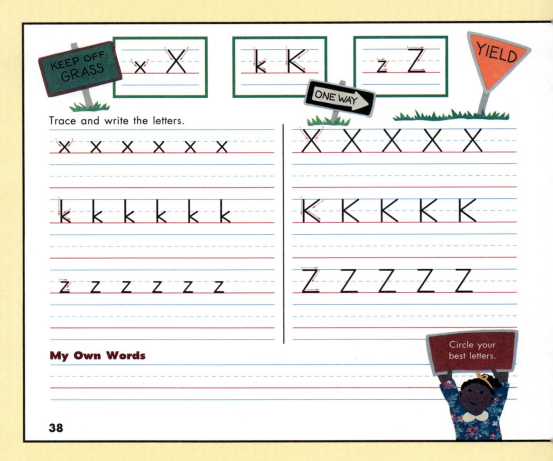

Trace and write the letters.

My Own Words

## MODEL THE WRITING

Write **x**, **k**, and **z** on guidelines as you say the stroke descriptions for each letter. Have students use their fingers to trace the models of these letters in their books as you repeat the descriptions. Follow the same procedure with **X**, **K**, and **Z**.

## A CLOSER LOOK

Call attention to the size and shape of the letters by asking questions such as these:
Which letters are short?
Which letters are tall?
Which letters are alike except for size?
Which letters begin with a slide right stroke?
Which letters have a pull down straight stroke?

## PRACTICE

Let students practice writing the letter pairs **xX**, **kK**, and **zZ** on laminated writing cards or slates before they write on the pages.

## EVALUATE

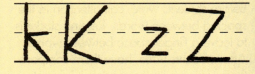

To help students evaluate their writing, ask questions such as these:
Do your slant strokes in **x** cross halfway between the midline and baseline?
Do your slant strokes in **X** cross at the midline?
Do your two slant strokes in **k** meet halfway between the midline and baseline?
Do your two slant strokes in **K** meet at the midline?
Do your **z** and **Z** rest on the baseline?

## BETTER LETTERS

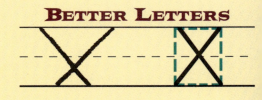

To ensure correct letter width, have students write the letter **x** or **X** and enclose it in a rectangle.

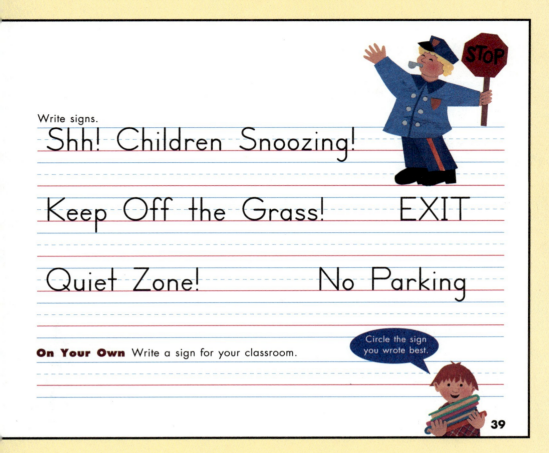

Write signs.

# Shh! Children Snoozing!

# Keep Off the Grass!     EXIT

# Quiet Zone!     No Parking

**On Your Own** Write a sign for your classroom.

Circle the sign you wrote best.

39

## WRITE LEGIBLY

Before students write, call attention to the finger space between the words.

After students write, have them compare their word spacing with that of the models. Guide students to recognize why one sign they wrote might be better than another.

## COACHING HINT

Review uppercase letters with slant strokes. Write **M, N, W, V, X,** and **K** on the chalkboard. Have students choose two letters to compare. Ask these questions: *How are they alike? How are they different? Which strokes are the same? Which letter has more strokes?* Repeat with circle letters **O, C, Q,** and **G** or straight line letters **L, I, T, E, F,** and **H**. (visual)

## PRACTICE MASTERS 47–52

Trace and write.
x  x  x  x  x  x  x  x  x
ax   six   fox   extra   fixes
tax   mix   boxes   exercise
Write your own words.
Name
Copyright © Zaner-Bloser, Inc.

Trace and write.
X  X  X  X  X  X  X  X  X
Xavier opened a surprise box
Xavier saw six more boxes

Trace and write.
k  k  k  k  k  k  k  k
keep   kept   king   know   talk
kiss   knife   kite   kitten   walk
Write your own words.
Name
Copyright © Zaner-Bloser, Inc.

Trace and write.
K  K  K  K  K  K  K
Kesse knows all about making kites
Kara learned about fixing bikes

Trace and write.
z  z  z  z  z  z  z  z
zoo   zone   zipped   buzzed
puzzle   zebra   pizza   maze
Write your own words.
Name
Copyright © Zaner-Bloser, Inc.

Trace and write.
Z  Z  Z  Z  Z  Z  Z  Z
Zebras' stripes zig and zag
Bees zip and buzz as they fly
Write something else you know about zebras.
Name
Copyright © Zaner-Bloser, Inc.     PRACTICE MASTER 52

## CONTINUOUS STROKE

Touch the headline; slant right to the baseline. Lift. Move to the right and touch the headline; slant left to the baseline.

Touch the headline; pull down straight to the baseline. Lift. Move to the right and touch the headline; slant left to the midline. Slant right to the baseline.

Touch the headline; slide right. Slant left to the baseline. Slide right.

## Write Away

**Who's at the Zoo?**
Invite students to write a story about a yak, a zebra, and a kangaroo who live at the zoo and are friends. Suggest they draw a picture to accompany their story and include signs that might be found at the zoo. (visual, kinesthetic)

Remind students they have been writing names of people, places, and things and titles of books and songs. Review the use of uppercase letters to begin names and important words in titles. Read the directions together.

## PRACTICE

Let students practice writing words on laminated writing cards or slates before they write on the pages.

---

**Evaluation**

# Show What You Can Do

Write some names you like.

Write the title of a movie you would like to see.

Write the title of a song you sing in school.

Write the title of a book you read.

Write a sign you might see in a school library.

Circle your best word.

40

---

## EVALUATE

To help students evaluate their writing, ask questions such as these:
Do your tall letters touch the headline and rest on the baseline?
Do your short letters touch the midline?
Are your letters straight up and down?
Are the letters in your words spaced correctly?

Draw a picture of a place you would like to visit.
Then write a story to go with your picture.

Put a star next to your best sentence.

41

## WRITE LEGIBLY

Before students write, encourage a lively sharing of ideas about different places they might choose for their pictures and story writing. You might want to list their suggestions on the chalkboard.

Remind students to begin each sentence with an uppercase letter and to use an end mark.

After they write, have students put a star beside their best sentence and tell why they chose it as their best.

Ask students to share their pictures and stories.

Certificates of Progress *should be awarded to those students who show notable handwriting progress and* Certificates of Excellence *to those who progress to the top levels of handwriting proficiency.*

## HANDWRITING AND THE WRITING PROCESS

Have students use the following steps to complete the page.

**Prewriting**
What should I write about?

**Drafting**
I write my ideas in sentences.

**Revising**
What should I change?

**Editing**
How can I improve my handwriting and spelling?

**Publishing**
How will I share my work?

### A Place Called Storyland

Ask students to imagine a place called Storyland, where characters from many different story books live. Distribute large sheets of drawing paper and crayons or markers, and have students title the page "Storyland." Ask them to draw a picture to show what Storyland looks like and what characters live there. Suggest they include favorite characters from books and movies.

### Be the Teacher

In advance, prepare a chart with sentences that include names and titles written with obvious errors in capitalization. Choose one student to be the "teacher." For each sentence, have the teacher choose a volunteer to come to the chart, tell what is wrong with that sentence, and explain how it might be corrected. Then ask the teacher to choose another student to rewrite the sentence correctly on the chalkboard. (visual, auditory)

Before You Go On . . .

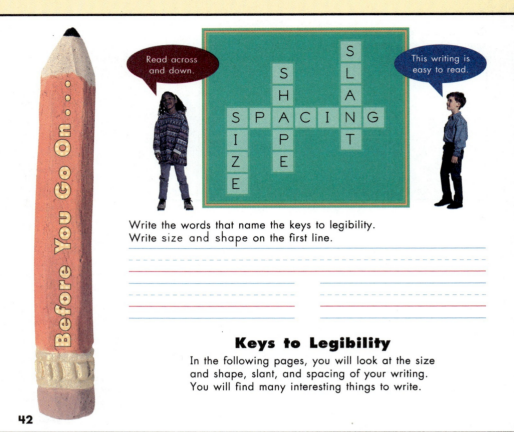

Read across and down.

This writing is easy to read.

Write the words that name the keys to legibility.
Write size and shape on the first line.

## Keys to Legibility

In the following pages, you will look at the size and shape, slant, and spacing of your writing. You will find many interesting things to write.

Use this page to introduce students to the **Keys to Legibility** section of the book. After students write the words that name the keys to legibility, discuss the content of this section.

### PREVIEW

Preview this section by calling attention to these features:
- models for writing words
- guidelines for writing
- opportunities for evaluating writing
- **On Your Own** activities with directions for independent writing

### PRACTICE MASTERS FOR THE KEYS TO LEGIBILITY

- Letter to Parents—English, 60
- Letter to Parents—Spanish, 61
- Certificates, 55–57
- Write in Spanish, 72–90
- Write in Japanese, 91–93
- Record of Student's Handwriting Skills, 54
- Zaner-Bloser Handwriting Grid, 94

## Keys to Legibility: Size and Shape

Make your writing easy to read.
Look at the size and shape of your letters.

hamster  rabbit  goldfish  cat

Write these words. Make sure your tall letters touch the headline.

lion  bear  zebra  mouse

Write these words. Make sure your short letters touch the midline.

jaguar  penguin  quail

Are your words easy to read?

Write these words. Make sure letters that go below
the baseline touch the next line.

43

---

## KEYS TO LEGIBILITY: SIZE AND SHAPE

In the pages that follow, students concentrate on size and shape and evaluate their writing for these qualities.

## MODEL THE WRITING

Write words that include tall letters and short letters as well as several letters with descenders. Have volunteers take turns naming a letter and noting its placement on the guidelines. Remind students that writing letters with correct size and shape will help make their writing easy to read.

## EVALUATE

lion

To help students evaluate the size and shape of their writing, ask questions such as these:
Look at the word *hamster*. Do your tall letters touch the headline?
Look at the word *lion*. Do your short letters touch the midline?
Look at the word *jaguar*. Do your **j** and **g** touch the next headline?

## COACHING HINT

To call attention to the part of a letter that descends below the baseline, write **g, j, p, q,** and **y** on guidelines on the chalkboard. Have students trace the descenders with colored chalk to highlight shape and placement on the guidelines. Point out where the letters touch the next headline. (visual, kinesthetic)

Write the following rhyme on chart paper and read it with the students.

## My Cat

My cat sleeps when the
  warm sun shines,
Then stretches and wanders
  about.
I call his name, but he
  doesn't come,
Even when I really shout!

Begin a discussion about cats by sharing these facts: An adult male tiger is a cat that can weigh 400 pounds. The average house cat weighs from 6 to 15 pounds.

Then invite students to share information about cats before they write about them.

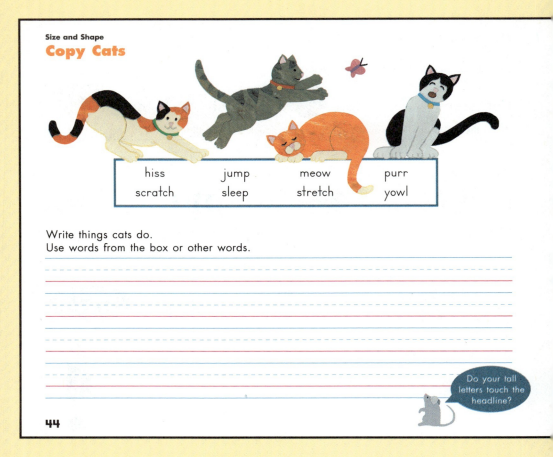

### Size and Shape
### Copy Cats

| hiss | jump | meow | purr |
| scratch | sleep | stretch | yowl |

Write things cats do.
Use words from the box or other words.

Do your tall letters touch the headline?

44

## EVALUATE

Remind students that writing letters the correct size and shape increases legibility. Suggest they look at their tall letters.

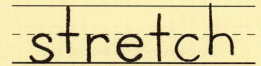

stretch

To help students evaluate the size of their tall letters, ask them to focus on a word with a tall letter. Then ask questions such as these:
Which tall letters are in the word you wrote?
Do your tall letters touch the headline?
Do your tall letters rest on the baseline?

## SIZE AND SHAPE

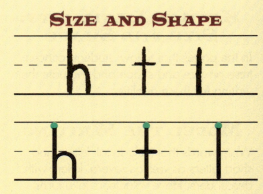

To help students improve their tall letters, draw a dot at the starting point of a letter. Have students use this starting point as they practice writing each letter.

**On Your Own**
What do you think cats like to do most? Write about it.

Circle your best word.

45

## WRITE LEGIBLY
Before students write, remind them to pay attention to the size and shape of letters. After students write, have them circle their best word and tell why they chose that word as their best.

## HANDWRITING AND THE WRITING PROCESS
This page asks students to write informatively about cats. For prewriting, invite the class to describe the daily activities of cats they know. As students talk, you may wish to write key words in a web that students can refer to as they write. Words from page 44 may be included.

To complete the writing process, have students revise and edit their drafts, checking spelling, punctuation, and handwriting. To publish the final drafts, ask a local pet store or animal shelter to display them along with students' photographs and illustrations of cats.

## COACHING HINT
Using guidelines on the chalkboard, write a line of tall letters with obvious errors in size. Have students take turns correcting the errors at the chalkboard. (visual, kinesthetic)

# Write Away

### Pet Names
Ask students to share the names of their pets. Discuss how owners sometimes name their pets based on special characteristics, for example, *Tangerine* for an orange- colored cat or *Mischief* for a naughty little kitten. Then ask students to write a list of pets and interesting names for each one. (visual)

Tangerine

# Fun and Games

### Buzz
Play a variation of the game "Buzz." Have students sit in a circle and take turns naming the lowercase letters of the alphabet in order. Tell them to substitute the word *buzz* for any tall lowercase letter, for example, "a, buzz, c, buzz," and so on. (visual, auditory)

Write the following poem on chart paper and read it with students.

### My Hero
I think I'll make a
   sandwich.
It will be my treat.
I'll put in lots of good
   things,
And then I'll sit and eat!

Begin a discussion about sandwiches by sharing this information:

It is believed that sandwiches were named after the Earl of Sandwich, who lived in England in the 1700s. It is said that he would order beef served to him between two slices of bread.

Ask students to name familiar kinds of breads, pointing out that bread is eaten in nearly every country in the world. Read *Bread, Bread, Bread* by Ann Morris with the class. Then ask them to name foods they like to eat in sandwiches.

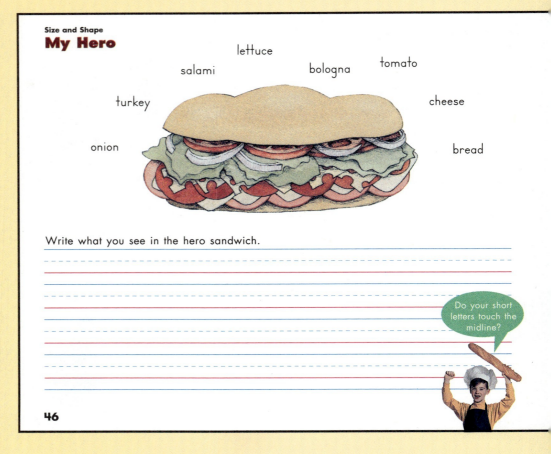

**Size and Shape**
**My Hero**

lettuce
salami
bologna
tomato
turkey
cheese
onion
bread

Write what you see in the hero sandwich.

Do your short letters touch the midline?

46

## EVALUATE
Remind students that writing letters the correct size and shape increases legibility. Suggest they look at their short letters.

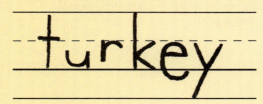

turkey

To help students evaluate the size of their short letters, ask them to focus on one word. Then ask questions such as these:
Which short letters are in the word you wrote?
Do your short letters touch the midline?
Do your short letters rest on the baseline?
Do any short letters go below the baseline and touch the next headline?

## SIZE AND SHAPE

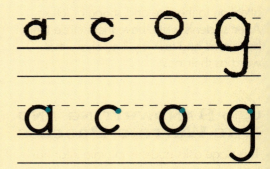

a c o g

a c o g

To help students improve short letters that begin below the midline with a backward circle, draw a dot to indicate the starting point of a letter. Have students use this starting point as they practice writing each letter. For the letter **o**, remind students not to let their eyes follow the pencil but to focus on the ending point of the letter.

## On Your Own
Tell how you would make a hero sandwich.

Circle your best word.

47

### Write Away

**Food and Fun**
Brainstorm with students a list of special events at which food is usually served, such as birthdays, picnics, holidays, and fairs. Assign partners. Ask them to choose an event and discuss what happens and what foods might be served. Then invite them to draw a picture showing the event, including labels for each of the foods shown. Have them display and describe their work. (visual, auditory)

### Fun and Games

**What's in the Basket?**
Draw the outline of a large picnic basket on the chalkboard and add guidelines. Give clues to identify a food and ask a student to name it and to write it on the basket. Classmates can help with spelling. After the student writes, ask a volunteer to name the short and tall letters and to tell where each letter begins and ends. Erase the word and start again. (auditory, visual)

### WRITE LEGIBLY
Before students write, remind them to pay attention to the size and shape of letters by focusing on the placement of letters on the guidelines.

After students write, have them circle their best word and tell why they chose that word as their best.

### COACHING HINT
Continue to use the chalkboard for teaching and practicing basic strokes, letters, and numerals. Students who have difficulty with their motor skills may benefit from the increased space the chalkboard provides. Since erasing is easy, identification and correction of errors becomes a simple task. (kinesthetic)

spaghetti

47

Write the following poem on the chalkboard or on chart paper and read it with students.

### Frogs and Toads
Are you a frog,
Or are you a toad?
Will you play in the water,
Or hop down the road?

Compare frogs and toads by sharing these facts:

- Both toads and frogs are amphibians. Amphibians are animals that can live both on land and in water.

- Toads live mainly on land but return to the water to mate and give birth. Frogs live mainly in water.

- Toads have skin that is rough and dry to touch. Frogs have skin that is moist and smooth.

Invite students to share other information they know about frogs and toads before they write.

48

---

Size and Shape
## Frogs and Toads

fire-bellied toad

duck-billed frog

painted reed frog

golden frog

Write the name of each frog and toad.

Does each g go below the baseline?

48

---

## EVALUATE

Remind students that writing letters with correct size and shape increases legibility. Suggest they look at letters that go below the baseline.

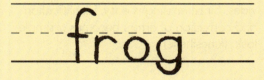

To help students evaluate their writing of letters with descenders, ask them to focus on the word frog. Ask questions such as these:

Does your **g** go below the baseline and touch the next headline?

Does your **g** curve and end just above the next headline?

## SIZE AND SHAPE

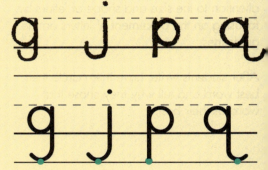

To help students improve letters with descenders, place a dot on the next headline to mark where the descender should touch. Have students aim for this mark as they practice writing each letter.

### On Your Own

Make up a name for this frog. Write a story about its life.

Circle your best word.

49

### About Frogs and Toads

Read to students from one of the *Frog and Toad* books by Arnold Lobel. Then invite students to write and illustrate their own adventures for Frog and Toad. Or assign partners and have them use nonfiction sources to find information on the differences between frogs and toads. Provide a chart for them to complete with their findings. (auditory, visual, kinesthetic)

FROGS | TOADS

# Fun and Games

### G Go Round

Invite students to sit in a circle. Play music and have students pass around a glove and a bag until the music stops. Ask the student holding the glove to write a word that begins with **g** on guidelines on the chalkboard. Ask the student with the bag to write a word that ends with **g**. After the game, have all the students write the words from the board. (auditory, visual, kinesthetic)

# Write Legibly

Before students write, remind them to pay attention to the size and shape of letters.

After students write, have them circle their best word and tell why they chose that word as their best.

Note: Illustration shows a tomato frog.

# Handwriting and The Writing Process

Thinking about legibility should always be part of the editing stage of the writing process. The **Keys to Legibility**—size and shape, slant, and spacing—help students know what to look for.

To check size and shape, students can compare their letters to the alphabet chart inside the back cover of their books. They should ask themselves:
Do my short letters touch the midline?
Do my tall letters touch the headline?
Did I use complete circles and lines?

# Coaching Hint

For students who are still confused about the direction in which to write the loop of the descender in the letters **g** and **q**, provide aluminum foil for them to use to shape the letters and then have them trace each letter with their fingers. Ask students to write the letters three times each, using the foil letter as a model. (kinesthetic)

Write the following on the chalkboard and read it with your class.

**Word Fun**
Down words,
Across words,
Covering-the-board words.
Short words, long words,
Do you know the cross-
    words?

Invite students to name the different kinds of word puzzles they have seen.

---

## Word Fun

Follow the directions to complete the word box.

1. Write f in box 1.
2. Write p in box 9.
3. Write a in box 4.
4. Write i in box 8.
5. Write n in box 3.
6. Write r in box 7.
7. Write a in box 6.
8. Write u in box 2.
9. Leave box 5 blank.

| 1 f | 2 u | 3 n |
|---|---|---|
| 4 a | 5 | 6 a |
| 7 r | 8 i | 9 p |

Are your letters easy to read?

Read across and down.
Write the four words you have spelled.

~~fun~~ ~~far~~

~~nap~~ ~~rip~~

50

---

Direct students' attention to the word puzzle on page 50. Discuss the directions for completing the puzzle.

## WRITE LEGIBLY

Before students write the letters in the boxes, remind them to write neatly and to think about the size and shape of the letters as they write.

After students write, go over the answers together.

Use the letters to write as many words as you can.

a  b  d  e  i  n  s  t  u

What words can you make from the letters in your name?

51

### From Words to Stories
Challenge students to use several of the words they wrote on page 51 to write an original story on a topic of their choice. (visual)

### Just the Opposite
Assign students to teams of three or four. Ask one student to be the note taker. Challenge the teams to name and list as many pairs of opposites as they can. At the end of a given time period, collect the lists and compare them. Give points for any opposite pair written correctly. The team with the most points wins. (auditory)

Direct students' attention to page 51. Tell them letters may be used more than once in a single word.

After students write, have them compare lists.

## COACHING HINT
Students who have mastered the skill of writing uppercase and lowercase letters without models should be given writing activities that challenge them. Reteaching, for any student who still needs it, is most effective if practice is given in the student's dominant modality.

Possible Answers:
tin, bin, din, in
nest, best, test
bad, sad
ten, den, Ben
bun, nun, sun
dent, bent, sent
tab, dab
but, nut
bed, Ted

Share the alphabet soup rhyme on the page with your students.

Ask students to name something to put in alphabet soup that begins with the letter **A**. Ask a volunteer to write the letter on guidelines on the chalkboard. Say the stroke descriptions as the student writes. Repeat with several other letters. Discuss the size and shape of the letters.

## FᴜN and GameS

### Name and Frame It!
Make monogrammed frames using alphabet macaroni letters, white glue, and craft sticks. Demonstrate how to make a frame by gluing wooden craft sticks together to form a rectangle.

Have students complete their frames and label them with their names spelled in alphabet macaroni letters. Frames may be painted with thinned tempera paint. When the frames are finished, use them to frame a good handwriting sample or a self-portrait. (kinesthetic, visual)

My name is Melissa.

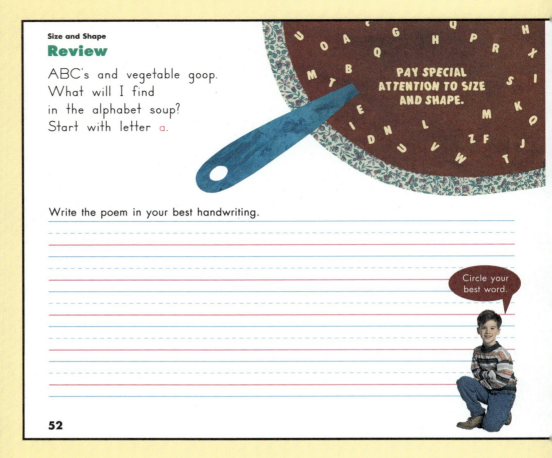

**Size and Shape**
### Review

ABC's and vegetable goop.
What will I find
in the alphabet soup?
Start with letter a.

PAY SPECIAL ATTENTION TO SIZE AND SHAPE.

Write the poem in your best handwriting.

Circle your best word.

52

## WRITE LEGIBLY

Before students write, remind them to pay attention to their use of guidelines.

After students write, have them circle their best word and tell why they chose that word as their best.

## COACHING HINT

Use chalk or masking tape to make large sets of guidelines on the playground or on the floor. Assign partners to each set. One student names a letter while the other hops, jumps, or tiptoes the shape of the letter on the guidelines. (auditory, kinesthetic)

**Keys to Legibility:** Slant

Make your writing easy to read.
Look at the slant of your letters.

**left hand**

**right hand**

1. Position your paper properly.
2. Pull downstrokes in the right direction.
3. Shift your paper as you write.

Write these words.
Make sure your pull down straight strokes are straight up and down.

 imagine    think    talk    write

 read    giggle    build

Are your words easy to read?

53

# KEYS TO LEGIBILITY: SLANT

In the pages that follow, students concentrate on correct slant and evaluate their writing for this quality.

## MODEL THE WRITING

Model the hints for good vertical quality as students follow along.

*Position your paper properly.*
- right-handed writer: straight
- left-handed writer: slanted left

*Pull downstrokes in the proper direction.*
- right-handed writer: toward the midsection
- left-handed writer: toward the left elbow

*Shift your paper as you write.*

Remind students that writing letters straight up and down, with correct slant, will help make their writing easy to read.

## EVALUATE

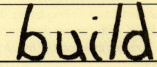
build

To help students evaluate the slant of their letters, ask questions such as these:
Look at the word *imagine*. Are the pull down straight strokes in **i, m, a, g, i,** and **n** straight up and down?
Look at the word *build*. Is the pull down straight stroke in each letter straight up and down?

## COACHING HINT

Practicing pull down straight strokes at the chalkboard is a good way to help students improve verticality. If students make the first stroke in a letter straight, the rest of the letter is more likely to be straight. Have the students use soft, oversized chalk. You may want to begin by placing sets of two dots about six inches apart to mark the starting and stopping point of each vertical stroke. (visual, kinesthetic)

## BEFORE WRITING

Read aloud the following rhyme.

### Clowns

Here come the clowns!
Some with frowns,
Some with smiles
That stretch for miles,
With baggy pants and big
  red nose
And water squirted from a
  rose.
I laugh at all the funny
  clowns,
With all their ups and all
  their downs.

Begin a discussion about clowns by sharing these facts:

There have always been people who dress up to make other people laugh. They have been known as jesters, jokers, and clowns. The clowns of today are known for their costumes and brightly painted faces.

Clowns, usually seen as part of circus troupes, are also part of rodeo performances where, besides making people laugh, they have the important job of distracting the bull from fallen riders.

Invite students to share other information about clowns.

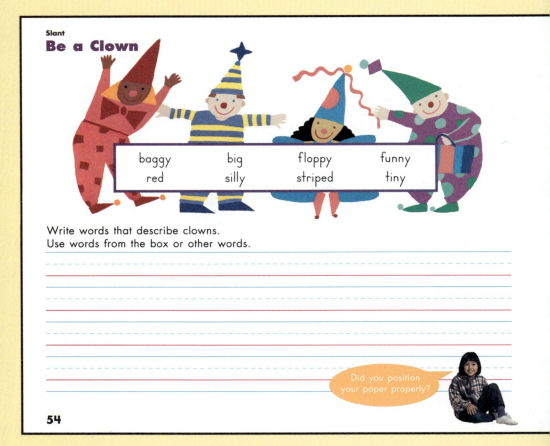

**Slant**
## Be a Clown

| baggy | big | floppy | funny |
| red | silly | striped | tiny |

Write words that describe clowns.
Use words from the box or other words.

Did you position your paper properly?

54

## EVALUATE

Remind students that writing letters straight up and down, with correct slant, increases legibility. Suggest they look at the slant of their letters.

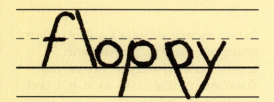

To help students evaluate the slant of their letters, ask them to focus on one word at a time and ask questions such as these:
Look at the word *floppy*. Are the pull down straight strokes in **f**, **l**, and **p** straight up and down?
Look at the word *striped*. Are the pull down straight strokes in **t**, **r**, **i**, **p**, and **d** straight up and down?

## SLANT

To help students improve the vertical quality of their letters, have them practice writing pull down straight strokes on guidelines. Mark the starting point and the stopping point with dots. Have students practice pull down straight strokes, beginning at the headline or midline and ending at the baseline or next headline.

**On Your Own**

If you dressed like a clown, what would you look like?
Draw a picture and describe it.

Circle a word in which your letters are straight up and down.

55

## Write Away

**Masquerade**
Explain to students that at a masquerade party, people dress in costumes. Discuss with students the kinds of costumes they might like to dress up in. Distribute manila paper and have students draw pictures of themselves in costumes. On another paper, have them write words that describe their costumes. Display the pictures, and call on volunteers to read their lists while their classmates try to identify each costume by the words used to describe it. (visual, auditory, kinesthetic)

## Fun and Games

**As Silly As a Clown**
Help students develop an understanding of the use of similes. Brainstorm a list together. Here are some to begin:

    as silly as a clown
    as slow as a snail
    as hungry as a bear
    as gentle as a kitten
    as quiet as a clam

Have students cut pictures from magazines or draw pictures of animals or people in action and then label them with an appropriate simile. (visual)

## WRITE LEGIBLY

Before students draw and write, remind them to check their paper position. As they write, remind them to shift their papers as the writing line fills.

**left hand**

**right hand**

After students write, have them circle a word with letters that are straight up and down and tell why they chose that word as their best.

## COACHING HINT

Correct paper placement is a factor for legibility. Check this periodically with each student. Remind students to check their paper placement whenever they write.

## HANDWRITING AND THE WRITING PROCESS

This page asks students to draw as a prewriting strategy. Making a detailed drawing before writing provides a visual reference that helps students include descriptive details when they write. As students draw, ask questions such as these:
What do your shoes look like?
Are you wearing a hat?

To complete the writing process, have students revise and edit their drafts, checking spelling, punctuation, and handwriting. After students complete a final copy of their descriptions and illustrations, publish their work in a class book.

**55**

Share the following poem with students.

**My Piñata**
See my piñata dance.
How it twirls in the sun!
Hit! Bang! Crash!
Treats for everyone!

Begin a discussion about piñatas by sharing these facts:

Piñatas are popular at fiestas, or parties, in Spain and South America. They are often made with papier-mâché and may be shaped like an animal. Small candies and toys are placed inside. Guests are blindfolded and take turns hitting the piñata with a stick until it breaks and its contents spill out. Then everyone dashes for the goodies.

Invite students to share any experiences they may have had with piñatas. If possible, have a piñata on hand for lots of fun!

---

Slant
## Inside Out

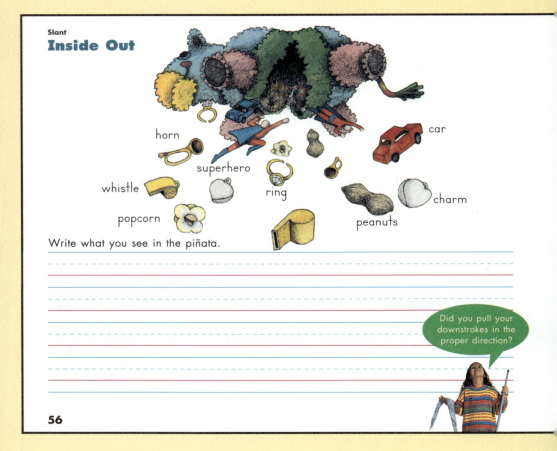

horn
car
superhero
whistle
ring
charm
popcorn
peanuts

Write what you see in the piñata.

Did you pull your downstrokes in the proper direction?

56

---

## EVALUATE

Remind students that writing letters that are straight up and down increases legibility. Suggest they look at letters with pull down straight strokes.

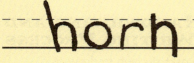

To help students evaluate the slant of their letters, ask them to focus on one word. Then ask questions such as these:
Which of your letters have pull down straight strokes?
Are your pull down straight strokes straight?
Do your pull down straight strokes start at the headline or midline?
Do your pull down straight strokes go straight to the baseline or through to the next headline?

## SLANT

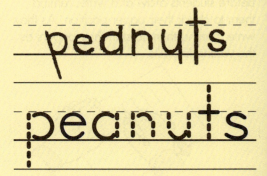

To help students improve the vertical quality of their letters, prepare letters for them to write with the pull down straight strokes highlighted with a dotted line. Have students practice letters with pull down straight strokes in this way.

## On Your Own
Write what you would put in a piñata.

Circle a word in which your letters are straight up and down.

57

**Birthday ABC**
Have students work in small groups to make Birthday ABC books. Distribute booklets with lined paper, one page for every letter of the alphabet. Have students follow these steps.

1. Print an upper and lowercase letter on each page.
2. Brainstorm an idea.
3. Write a sentence or phrase.
4. Illustrate the idea.

Here are some ideas:
Aa  An invitation
Bb  Birthday cake
Cc  Cards
Dd  Dressing up
Ee  Everyone singing
Ff  Friends and family
Gg  Good things to eat
(visual, auditory)

### WRITE LEGIBLY
Before students write, remind them to pay attention to the slant of their letters.

After students write, have them circle a word with letters that are straight up and down and tell why they chose that word as their best.

### HANDWRITING AND THE WRITING PROCESS
Legible handwriting is important during every stage of the writing process. During prewriting, students plan for their writing by making notes, lists, and webs. "Sloppy" prewriting work may cause confusion throughout the writing process, but easy-to-read notes and webs smooth the way for students, teachers, and writing partners.

Remind students to write legibly as they list items to put in a piñata. This activity might serve as prewriting for a longer piece.

### COACHING HINT
If the pull down straight strokes that students write slant in either direction, have them check the paper and reposition it if necessary. Remind right-handed writers to pull their downstrokes toward the midsection and left-handed writers to pull toward the left elbow. Tell students to relax the hold on their pencils. (visual, kinesthetic)

### FUN and GAMES

**Make a Piñata**
Turn a grocery-size paper bag into a piñata using streamers and other decorations. Invite students to write words on lined paper strips. Wrap and tape each word around a food or toy treat. Break the piñata, enjoy the treat, and have each word read aloud. (visual, kinesthetic)

Read the following poem to
your students.

**Creeping Crawlers**
Watch that little bug
As it begins to crawl
Slowly it creeps
Up the garden wall.
Does it have six legs
As all insects do?
Does it crawl along
Over, under, and through?

Compare different kinds of
insects using these facts:

• An insect is a small animal
  that has six legs. There
  are more insects on earth
  than any other kind of
  animal.

• The word *bug* is used to
  refer to insects of all different kinds, but bugs are
  only one type of insect.

• Another kind of insect is
  the beetle. The word
  *beetle* means "to bite."
  Beetles do enormous
  damage to the plants they
  feed on.

Invite students to write the
names of familiar insects
and display them on a
chart.

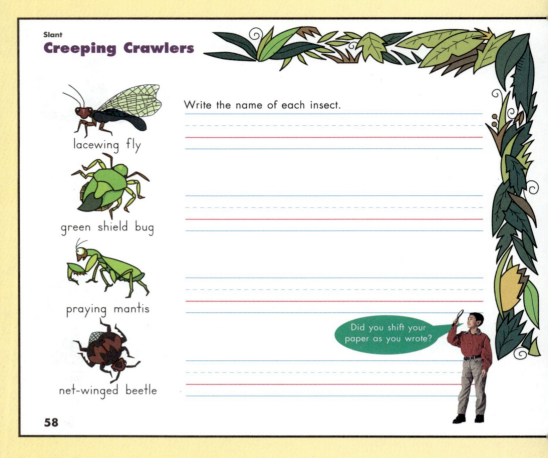

Slant
**Creeping Crawlers**

Write the name of each insect.

lacewing fly

green shield bug

praying mantis

Did you shift your
paper as you wrote?

net-winged beetle

58

## EVALUATE

Remind students that shifting the paper as
they write will help them write letters with
the straight up and down quality that
makes for good handwriting. Suggest they
look to see if their letters are straight up
and down.

To help students evaluate the slant of their
letters, ask them to focus on one word.
Then ask questions such as these:
Which letters have pull down straight
strokes?
Is the pull down straight stroke in each letter straight up and down?
Did you shift the paper as the writing line
filled?

## SLANT

To help students improve the vertical quality
of their letters, draw lightly over the pull
down straight strokes. If all the pencil lines
are parallel, the vertical quality is correct.

**On Your Own**

Imagine you are this insect. Tell what you do each day.

Circle a word in which your letters are straight up and down.

59

**Big Book of Insects**

Display nonfiction books with photographs and drawings of insects. Invite students to draw several insects, to label them, and to write about them using facts they already know or information from the books. Ask volunteers to work together to make a cover. Bind the pages to make a Big Book of Insects. (visual, kinesthetic)

Fun and Games

**A Spelling Bee**

Have a spelling bee using words from other curriculum areas. Divide students into two or more teams. Ask each player to spell and write a word on guidelines on the chalkboard. Let students determine whether or not a word is spelled correctly. Give one point for each correctly spelled word. The team with the most points wins. (auditory, kinesthetic)

## WRITE LEGIBLY

Before students write, remind them to shift their papers as their writing space fills and to pay attention to writing pull down straight strokes straight.

After students write, have them circle a word with letters that are straight up and down and tell why they chose that word as their best.

Note: Illustration shows a katydid.

## COACHING HINT

Draw writing lines on 9" x 12" pieces of oak tag and laminate one sheet for each student. Students can use these as "slates" to practice writing, using a wipe-off crayon. Have students practice one letter with pull down straight strokes. Remind them to shift the slate as they write. Have them continue with other letters. (kinesthetic)

## HANDWRITING AND THE WRITING PROCESS

Thinking about legibility should always be part of the editing stage of the writing process. The **Keys to Legibility**—size and shape, slant, and spacing—help students know what to look for.

To check the slant of their writing, students can draw faint pencil lines through several vertical line letters on a draft and check to make sure the lines are parallel. As they look at their writing, students should ask themselves:
Is my writing straight up and down?
Do any letters slant left or right?

Ask students to point to the different names for bread as you say each word and name the language.

Invite students to describe the breads pictured and to tell which kinds they have eaten.

Begin a brief discussion about bread by sharing these facts:

Bread is one of the most important foods in the world. Its main ingredients are flour and water. The most commonly used flour is wheat. Some breads are flat. Some breads are made with yeast, which makes them rise. Breads are sometimes filled or covered with fruits, vegetables, nuts, or meat.

## In Other Words

Write the words that name the baked food.

English
bread

German
brot

French
pain

Spanish
pan

English _____

German _____

French _____

Spanish _____

60

## WRITE LEGIBLY

Before students write, remind them to pay attention to the keys to legibility: size and shape, slant, and spacing. Ask students to check for correct paper placement and pencil position.

After students write, you may wish to go over the names once again.

*Practice Masters 72–90 provide practice in writing in Spanish.*

Italian
pane

Japanese
pan

Russian
khlep

Hebrew
lechem

Italian

Japanese

Russian

Hebrew

61

## COACHING HINT

Write *bread* on the chalkboard. Call attention to the letters **b** and **d** and ask how they are alike and how they are different. Remind students that if a circle in a letter comes before the pull down straight stroke, it is always a backward circle, as in **d**. If the pull down straight stroke in a letter comes before the circle, the circle is always a forward circle, as in **b**. (visual)

## Write Away

### It's Bread!
Write this web on the chalkboard:

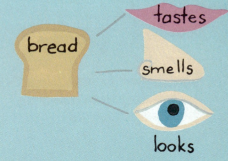

If available, show photographs of fresh bread, perhaps from a magazine or cookbook. Talk about the way bread tastes, smells, and looks. Ask students to copy the web and complete it with describing words. (visual, kinesthetic)

## Fun and Games

### Bake Some Bread
Invite someone who bakes bread to come to class and show your students how to make bread. Suggest that the students help with the kneading or braiding. Share the bread and ask students to describe its taste.

Culminate the activity by writing an experience chart together. Have students copy the chart and illustrate their writing. (auditory, visual, kinesthetic)

Read the jump-rope chant on the page to your students. Invite students to read it in groups. Ask one group to recite the first and third lines and the other to recite the second and fourth lines.

Call attention to the rhythm pattern. Ask students to clap the rhythm as you read the chant again.

## FuN and GameS

### Just One More

Say three or four words that are alike in some way. For example, the words might begin with the same letter, end with the same letter, contain the same medial vowel sound, rhyme, have like meanings, or belong to another category of words. When a student discovers in what way they are alike, he or she should show it by writing another word on the chalkboard that belongs in the set. That student can then begin the next round by naming another group of three words. (auditory, visual, kinesthetic)

**62**

---

Slant

## Review

Jump rope, jump rope,
Just watch this!
Jump rope, jump rope,
I can't miss!

Pay special attention to slant.

Write the poem in your best handwriting.

Circle a word in which your letters are straight up and down.

62

## WRITE LEGIBLY

Before students write, remind them to write letters that are straight up and down.

After students write, have them circle their best word and tell why they chose that word as their best.

## COACHING HINT

To review vertical slant, point out that it is important to make the first stroke in the letter straight. Write the following letters on guidelines and then make copies for the students: h, i, j, k, l, m, n, p, r, t, u, B, D, E, F, H, I, J, K, L, M, N, P, R, T, U. Have students trace over the pull down straight strokes with colored pencils and then write the letters. (visual, kinesthetic)

## Keys to Legibility: Spacing

Make your writing easy to read.
Look at the spacing between letters and words.

These letters are too close.

Miguel

These letters are too far apart.

Mary

Write these names.
Make sure your spacing is just right.

Samuel

Teiko

There should be a finger space between words. Write the sentence.

Miguel and Mary read rhymes.

Is your sentence easy to read?

63

---

## KEYS TO LEGIBILITY: SPACING

In the pages that follow, students concentrate on correct spacing between letters and words and evaluate their writing for this quality.

## MODEL THE WRITING

On guidelines on the chalkboard, write the name of one of your students. First write it with letters that are too close, then with letters that are too far apart. Ask a volunteer to explain why each is incorrect and to rewrite the name correctly. Remind students that writing with correct spacing between letters, and between words, will help make their writing easy to read.

## EVALUATE

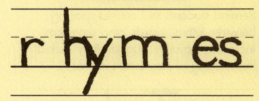

To help students evaluate the spacing in their writing, ask questions such as these: Look at the word *rhymes*. Are the letters in the word too close or too far apart? Is there room for a finger space between the words in your sentence?

## COACHING HINT

Remind students that there is a wider space between sentences than between words. Demonstrate how to place two fingers between sentences, and have students practice by writing a series of three short sentences. (kinesthetic, visual)

Write the following rhyme on the chalkboard and read it with students. Explain that a gander is a male goose.

Old Mother Goose,
When she wanted to
    wander,
Would ride through the air
On a very fine gander.

Begin a discussion of Mother Goose rhymes by sharing this information:

No one knows for sure whether there really was one person who was Mother Goose. Some people believe that Mother Goose may refer to a Mistress Elizabeth Goose who lived in Boston, Massachusetts, in the 1600s. She enjoyed reciting rhymes for her grandchildren, and these rhymes were collected by her son-in-law, a printer, who published them in 1719.

Have students recite familiar Mother Goose rhymes or read some to the class.

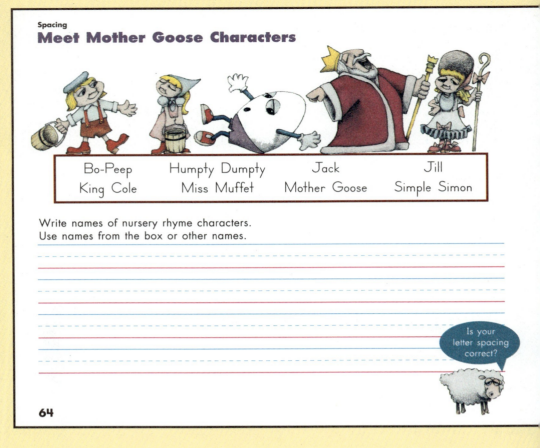

Spacing
## Meet Mother Goose Characters

| Bo-Peep | Humpty Dumpty | Jack | Jill |
|---|---|---|---|
| King Cole | Miss Muffet | Mother Goose | Simple Simon |

Write names of nursery rhyme characters.
Use names from the box or other names.

Is your letter spacing correct?

64

## EVALUATE

Remind students that correct spacing between letters, words, and sentences increases legibility. Suggest they look at the spacing of their letters in words.

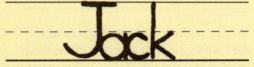

To help students evaluate the spacing of their letters in words, ask them to focus on the name *Jack.* Then ask questions such as these:
Do any of your letters touch each other?
Are your letters too far apart?
Does the spacing look just right?

## SPACING

To help students improve their spacing between words, demonstrate how to use an index finger to help create a finger space.

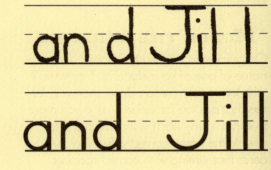

## On Your Own

Which nursery rhyme character would you like to meet? Tell why.

Circle a word with correct letter spacing.

65

## Mother Goose Rhymes

Invite students to write their favorite Mother Goose rhymes in their best handwriting and to draw pictures to accompany them. Make a book with their rhymes. Ask a kindergarten teacher if some of your students can visit and share the rhymes with kindergartners. (visual, auditory)

## Mother Goose Mysteries

Brainstorm a list of Mother Goose rhymes and write them on the chalkboard. Then give clues and ask students to identify the character being described. Have the student who guesses correctly write the name on guidelines on the chalkboard. Invite students to give riddle clues of their own. (auditory)

## WRITE LEGIBLY

Before students write, remind them to pay attention to the spacing between letters in words.

After students write, have them circle the word with the best spacing and tell why they chose it as their best.

## HANDWRITING AND THE WRITING PROCESS

This page asks students to write to inform. As a prewriting activity, recall familiar nursery rhymes by reading or reciting them aloud or inviting groups of students to act them out. Afterward, ask students to list details about their favorite nursery rhyme characters.

To complete the writing process, have students revise and edit their drafts, checking spelling, punctuation, and handwriting. Invite students to share their work by reading their final versions aloud to the class.

## COACHING HINT

Continue the use of the chalkboard for teaching and practicing the basic strokes in letters and spacing between letters in words. Students who have difficulty with their motor skills on paper may benefit from the increased space the chalkboard provides. Since erasing is easy, identification and correction of errors is a simple task. (kinesthetic)

Write the following poem on the chalkboard and read it together with students.

**The Best Nest**
Whose nest is best?
Now let me see.
The nest that is best
Is the one that's for me!

Begin a discussion about nests by sharing these facts.

Each bird of a species builds exactly the same kind of nest as other birds of its kind.
The female bird usually does the building and selects the location.

It usually takes about a week to build a nest.

Most nests are made from plant materials, such as twigs, fibers, and caterpillar silk.

Invite students to share any experiences they have had with bird nests before they write about them.

Spacing
## The Best Nest

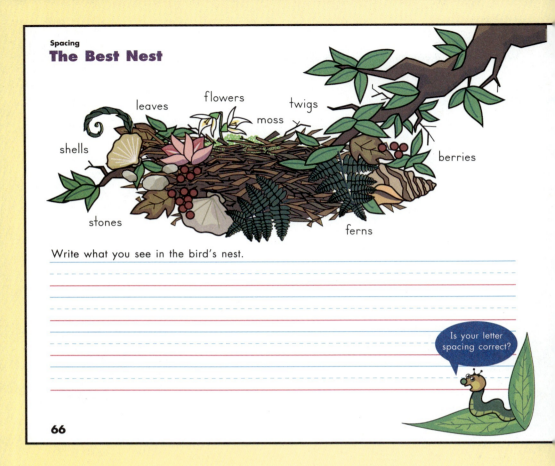

leaves    flowers    twigs
moss
shells
berries

stones    ferns

Write what you see in the bird's nest.

Is your letter spacing correct?

66

## EVALUATE

Remind students that writing words with correct letter spacing increases legibility. Suggest they look at the spacing of letters in their words.

To help students evaluate the spacing in their writing, ask them to focus on one word. Then ask questions such as these:
Are any of your letters too close together?
Are any of your letters too far apart?
Are the letters in your word spaced evenly?

## SPACING

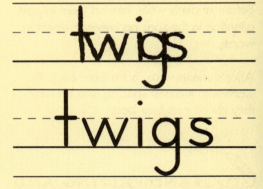

twigs

twigs

To help students understand letter spacing in words, show them a word with letters spaced too close together. Rewrite it correctly and have them practice writing the word below the model.

### On Your Own
Write what you would use to make a nest.

Circle a word with correct letter spacing.

**67**

## WRITE LEGIBLY

Before students write, remind them to pay attention to the spacing between letters in the words they write.

After students write, have them circle their word with the best letter spacing and tell why they chose that word as their best.

## COACHING HINT

A slate is good for practicing correct spacing between letters. Suggest students practice writing words on their slates before they write in their books or on paper. (kinesthetic)

### Birds and Their Nests

Invite students to work with a partner to get information about one kind of bird and its nest. Suggest they draw a picture, label the bird, and write a description of it. Encourage students to add information about the bird's habitat or usual activities. Allow time for students to share their findings. (visual, kinesthetic)

Cardinal

## FUN and GAMES

### Guess My Favorite

Most students have a favorite bird or other animal they like to draw, listen to stories about, or read about. Ask students to write a brief description of their favorite animal without naming it. Invite volunteers to read aloud their descriptions and have classmates guess the animal being described. (visual, auditory)

**67**

Write the following familiar poem on chart paper and read it with the students.

Once I saw a little bird
Come hop, hop, hop;
So I cried, "Little Bird,
Will you stop, stop, stop?"
I was going to the
    window
To say, "How do you do?"
But he shook his little tail
And far away he flew.

Begin a discussion by naming each bird and sharing these facts:

Cuckoo birds have a two-note song. Cuckoo clocks are named for the cuckoo bird.

Stilts use their long slender bills to search their muddy seaside home for food.

Puffins, or sea parrots, nest in seaside cliffs. They are very good at catching fish in their beaks.

Hornbills are tropical birds named for their long bills.

Page 69 shows a spoonbill, a long-legged wading bird named for its bill, which resembles a serving spoon.

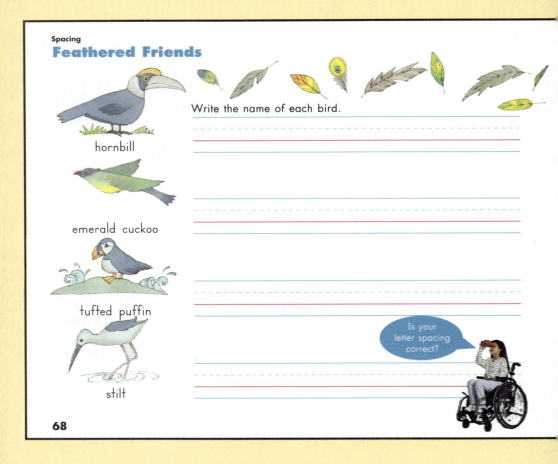

Spacing
## Feathered Friends

hornbill

emerald cuckoo

tufted puffin

stilt

Write the name of each bird.

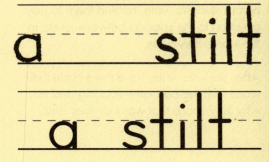

Is your letter spacing correct?

68

## EVALUATE

Remind students that writing words with correct letter spacing increases legibility. Suggest they look at their letter spacing.

horn bill

hornbill

To help students understand the importance of correct spacing, write *hornbill* on the chalkboard as shown in the first example above. Explain that because of the space between the two parts of the word, a reader might think the name is two words instead of one. Ask a volunteer to write the name correctly. Then have students look at their own writing and decide if the word *hornbill* has correct letter spacing.

## SPACING

a stilt

a stilt

To help students understand correct spacing between words, write *a stilt* as shown in the two examples above. Call attention to the space between words. Ask students to identify the correct model. Then ask them to write the words, leaving a finger space between them.

**On Your Own**
Describe this bird. Make up a name for it.

Put a star next to a sentence with good word spacing.

69

## All About Birds: A Dictionary

Give each student a card printed with a word that relates to birds, their nests, or their habits. Ask students to write a brief definition next to the word, using a dictionary for help. Students should add an illustration when appropriate. Collect the cards and ask volunteers to alphabetize them. Put them together to make a bird dictionary. Try this again for other subjects that interest your class. (visual, kinesthetic)

## WRITE LEGIBLY

Before students write, remind them to pay attention to the spacing of letters in words and between words.

After students write, have them circle the word with the best letter spacing and tell why they chose this word as their best.

Note: Illustration shows a roseate spoonbill.

## HANDWRITING AND THE WRITING PROCESS

Thinking about legibility should always be part of the editing stage of the writing process. The **Keys to Legibility**—size and shape, slant, and spacing—help students know what to look for.

To check their drafts for spacing, students can make sure there is about a one-finger space between words and about a two-finger space between sentences. Students should ask themselves:
Are any letters too close or too far apart?
Did I leave margins on my paper?
Did I indent each paragraph?

## COACHING HINT

For students who are having difficulty with letter formation and letter spacing, kinesthetic reinforcement might be helpful. Write words in large print on oak tag cards and apply glue and glitter to them. Let students trace the letters. Then have them trace the letters in the word again, noting the spacing between letters. (kinesthetic)

## Scrambled Eggs? No—Birds!

Write the names of different birds on the chalkboard with the letters in scrambled order. Have the students unscramble the letters, name the bird, and write each name on lined paper. Call on volunteers to write scrambled words for their classmates to decode. (visual)

einnightgal

Read the chant on the page with students. Ask them to imagine themselves jumping rope to this chant. Then ask on which word they think they might begin to jump faster and tell why.

Call attention to spacing between words. Point out the hyphen in *red-hot* and tell students to allow the same spacing as for a letter. Have them name each end mark they see.

Invite students to share other rhymes they know.

## FUN and GAMES

### Letters Into Words

Write these names of foods from the chant on the chalkboard:

salt    sugar    vinegar
mustard         pepper

Challenge students to use the letters from the words to write as many words as they can. Explain that repeating letters and changing them to uppercase letters for names is allowed. Provide dictionaries to help with spelling. Some students might benefit from having the letters printed on cards they can manipulate. Set a time limit and see how many different words the students have written.

**Spacing**
## Review

Mabel, Mabel, set the table,
Just as fast as you are able.
Salt, sugar, vinegar,
mustard, red-hot pepper!

*Pay special attention to spacing.*

Write the poem in your best handwriting.

*Put a star next to a line with good word spacing.*

70

## WRITE LEGIBLY

Before they write, remind students to use a finger space between words.

After students write, have them put a star next to a line they wrote with good word spacing and tell why they chose that line.

## COACHING HINT

Students' progress in handwriting is greater when short, intensive periods of instruction and review are used, approximately fifteen minutes daily.

**Keys to Legibility:** Size and Shape

Let's look at size and shape again.

dog    parrot    snail    newt

Write these words. Make sure your straight lines are straight.

_____

cow    goat    chick    duck

Write these words. Make sure your circle lines are round.

_____

gopher    porcupine    squirrel

Are your words easy to read?

Write these words.
Make sure lines that go below the baseline touch the next headline.

_____

71

---

# KEYS TO LEGIBILITY: SIZE AND SHAPE

In the pages that follow, students concentrate on correct size and shape and evaluate their writing for these qualities.

## MODEL THE WRITING

Review the strokes used to write manuscript letters—pull down straight, slide right and slide left, circle forward and circle backward, and slant right and slant left. Write several letters on guidelines on the chalkboard and ask students to identify the strokes used to form each letter. Remind them that writing letters with correct size and shape will help make their writing easy to read.

## EVALUATE

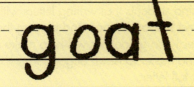

To help students evaluate the size and shape of their writing, ask questions such as these:
Look at the word *goat*. Is the pull down straight stroke in your **t** straight?
Is your **o** round?
Does your **g** touch the next headline?

## COACHING HINT

Help students use a ruler to draw horizontal lines along the tops of letters to show correct size. Have them use this technique to evaluate the size of their letters, especially when they are writing on paper without guidelines. (visual)

Read the following poem to
your students.

**A Dog's Life**
My dog is a pet who is
   loved very much,
He's cared for and petted
   and such;
Whatever he does, in his
   own playful way,
I know it's "I love you" he's
   trying to say.

Begin a discussion about
dogs by sharing these facts:

Dogs were the first animals
to be trained by humans.
Because they can be trained,
dogs are used for hunting,
herding animals, guarding,
and tracking. They can also
be trained to act as "eyes"
for people who are blind
and "ears" for those who
are deaf. Dogs are popular
pets throughout the world.

Continue the discussion by
having students share their
observations before they
write about dogs.

Size and Shape
**A Dog's Life**

| bark | beg | dig | fetch |
| growl | roll over | sniff | wag |

Write things dogs do.
Use words from the box or other words.

Do your tall
letters touch the
headline?

72

## EVALUATE

Remind students that writing letters with
correct size and shape and placing them
correctly on guidelines will help make their
writing easier to read. Suggest they look at
their tall letters.

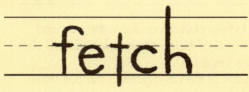

To help students evaluate their writing, ask
them to focus on one word with tall letters.
Then ask questions such as these:
Which tall letters are in the word you
wrote?
Do your tall letters touch the headline?
Do your tall letters rest on the baseline?
Are there pull down straight strokes in the
tall letters you wrote?

## SIZE AND SHAPE

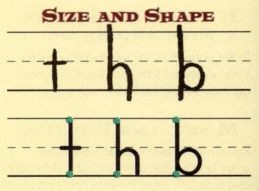

To help students improve their tall letters,
have them say the stroke descriptions as
they write a letter. Remind them to focus
on making pull down strokes straight and
beginning and ending them correctly on
the guidelines. Point out the retraces in **h**
and **b**.

**On Your Own**
What do you think dogs like to do most? Write about it.

Circle your best word.

73

**If They Could Talk**
Display an example of a cartoon with dialogue in speech balloons. Invite students to draw a cartoon showing two animals engaged in a conversation. Ask students to suggest what the animals might say to each other and to write their words in speech balloons. Students may continue by adding other scenes and dialogue. Display their cartoons. (visual)

**F**u**N** and **G**ame**S**

**Rhyme and Write**
Help students with rhyming by reading aloud the following phrases about animals:

a dog on a log
a flea that can ski
a monkey on a donkey
a quail on a trail
a giraffe with a laugh

Invite them to work in small groups and to write their own rhyming phrases on lined paper. Encourage them to use a dictionary for help with spelling. (auditory)

## WRITE LEGIBLY

Before students write, remind them to pay attention to the size and shape of letters.

After students write, have them circle their best word and tell why they chose that word as their best. Ask them to name the tall letters in the word and the strokes used to write them.

## HANDWRITING AND THE WRITING PROCESS

Legible handwriting is important during every stage of the writing process. Students' best handwriting isn't necessary for a first draft. In fact, concentrating on handwriting may take students' attention away from the content of their writing. However, a "sloppy" draft makes revising and editing more difficult. As students develop a consciousness about legibility, their writing will be fluent **and** easy to read.

Encourage students to write legibly as they write a first draft about dogs.

## COACHING HINT

For students who need additional practice with basic strokes, give each student a card on which one of the basic strokes is written. Tell students to write that stroke on lined paper and then to write all the tall uppercase and lowercase letters that contain that stroke. Students can trade cards and repeat the activity. (visual)

Write the following poem on chart paper and read it with students.

### Vegetable Soup

Put some vegetables in the
  pot, pot, pot.
Cook the soup till it's
  hot, hot, hot.
Stir and serve it,
  one, two, three.
Tasty soup for you and me.

Talk about ingredients that might be used to make soup, and share these facts:

Soup is a favorite food in countries around the world. Soup is water with other ingredients added. Barley is a grain used to thicken soup. Several vegetables are commonly added to soup. Carrots and onions grow underground. Celery grows above ground. Tomatoes, though sometimes referred to as vegetables, are the fruit of the plant. Lima beans are the seeds of a climbing plant.

Size and Shape
## Stone Soup

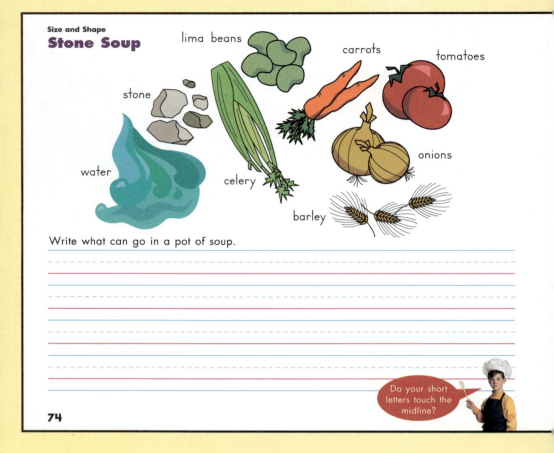

lima beans
carrots
tomatoes
stone
water
celery
onions
barley

Write what can go in a pot of soup.

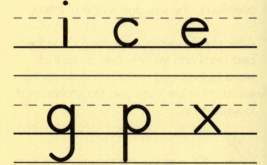

Do your short letters touch the midline?

74

## EVALUATE

Remind students that writing letters with correct size and shape increases legibility. Suggest they look at the shape of their letters.

**water**

To help students evaluate their writing, ask them to focus on the shape of the short letters in one word. Then ask questions such as these:
Which short letters are in the word you wrote?
Do your short letters touch the midline?
Do your short letters rest on the baseline?

## SIZE AND SHAPE

**i c e**

**g p x**

To review basic strokes, write the letters **i**, **c**, **e**, **g**, **p**, **x** on the chalkboard. Ask a student to trace each letter with a wet paintbrush while naming the strokes used. Be sure to point out the retrace strokes. Have students practice writing these and other short letters.

## On Your Own

Write what you would put in a pot of stone soup. Don't forget the stone!

Circle your best word.

75

**Illustrate *Stone Soup***
Share the story *Stone Soup* with your students. Talk about the ingredients used in the soup. Then have the class take turns retelling parts of the story as you write them on chart paper. Ask students to choose one sentence, write it on lined paper, cut it out, paste it to the bottom of drawing paper, and illustrate it. (auditory, visual)

# Fun and Games

**Let's Make Soup**
Prepare ahead for making stone soup in the classroom by developing a recipe on chart paper with the class. Then have students write notes to take home requesting an ingredient for the soup or equipment for cooking. Let students help prepare the vegetables. Place the vegetables in a pot of water, and add a clean stone, of course! Enjoy the results! At another time, have students copy the recipe to share with their families. (visual)

## Write Legibly

Before students write, remind them to pay attention to the size and shape of their letters.

After students write, have them circle their best word and tell why they chose that word as their best.

## Coaching Hint

For students who are still having difficulty forming letters, write a letter on guidelines on poster board or cardboard and laminate it. Students can use the letterforms as a base for making the letters with clay. Have students trace their completed letters and say the stroke descriptions. (kinesthetic, auditory, visual)

Ask students to find each animal pictured as you read these lines.

## Hairy Mammals

I'm a star-nosed mole
in a hole.
I'm a three-toed sloth
catching a moth.
I'm a duck-billed platypus
making such a fuss.
I'm a wrinkle-faced bat.
Imagine that!
We are hairy mammals!

Share facts about these unusual mammals.

Moles spend most of their lives underground.

Platypuses live in lakes and streams in Australia.

Bats fly, and they use their legs and feet to hang onto things but not to walk.

Sloths live up high in the forests of Central and South America and rarely descend to the ground.

Size and Shape
### Hairy Mammals

duck-billed platypus

three-toed sloth

wrinkle-faced bat

star-nosed mole

Write the name of each mammal.

Does each p go below the baseline?

76

## EVALUATE

Remind students that some short letters have strokes that go below the baseline and touch the next headline.

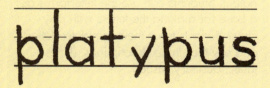

To help students evaluate the letters **p** and **y,** ask questions such as these:
Does your **p** begin at the midline?
Does your **p** go below the baseline and touch the next headline?
Does your **y** go below the baseline and touch the next headline?

## SIZE AND SHAPE

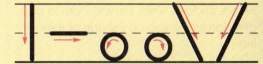

To help students improve the shape of their letters, review the basic strokes by writing them on the chalkboard. Have students use colored chalk to trace over them.

## On Your Own
Write about how this mammal might protect itself.

Circle your best word.

77

## WRITE LEGIBLY

Before students write, remind them to pay attention to the size and shape of letters.

After students write, have them circle their best word and tell why they chose that word as their best.

Note: Illustration shows hairy armadillo.

### ✏️ HANDWRITING AND THE WRITING PROCESS

Thinking about legibility should always be part of the editing stage of the writing process. The **Keys to Legibility**—size and shape, slant, and spacing—help students know what to look for.

To check size and shape, students can compare their letters to the alphabet chart in the back of their books. They should ask themselves:
Do my short letters touch the midline?
Do my tall letters touch the headline?
Did I use complete circles and lines?

## COACHING HINT

On the chalkboard, demonstrate forming the letters with descenders **g, j, p, q, y**. Ask which ones end on the headline of the next writing space and which curve up and end just above it. Have students trace each descender with colored chalk to highlight its shape and size. (visual)

## Write Away

### Weird and Wonderful
On the chalkboard, write the names of the mammals from the student page. Explain that each name helps to describe the animal by giving information about it. Then write a list of mammal names on the chalkboard, preceded by two blank lines, for example:

_____ _____ bear
_____ _____ fox

Have students work with partners to write descriptive animal names. Allow time for sharing the new names. (auditory, visual)

## Fun and Games

### Missing Letters
Write the following list on the chalkboard.

g _ _ s e
g i r a _ _ e
d _ _ r
_ _ r d v a r k
a _ _ i g a t o r
b a b _ _ n
b u _ _ a l o
g o r i _ _ a
k a n g a r _ _

Tell students that each animal name can be completed with double letters. Do the first one together, and then have students write the list and complete it independently. (visual)

77

Ask students to think about their favorite number as they listen to you read this poem aloud.

### Number Fun

What's your favorite number?
Is it 1 or 2?
Maybe it's 27.
Maybe it's 32.
Maybe it's your birthday,
Or maybe it tells your age,
Or maybe it's the number
You see right on this page!

Invite students to share their favorite numbers and to write the numerals on the chalkboard.

## Number Fun

Add the numbers to complete the number square.

| 1 | 2 | 3 | 4 | 5 | 6 | 7 | 8 | 9 | 10 | 11 | 12 | 13 | 14 |

| Add + | 9 | 8 | 7 | 6 | 5 |
|---|---|---|---|---|---|
| 1 | 10 | 9 | 8 | 7 | 6 |
| 2 | 11 | 10 | 9 | 8 | 7 |
| 3 | 12 | 11 | 10 | 9 | 8 |
| 4 | 13 | 12 | 11 | 10 | 9 |
| 5 | 14 | 13 | 12 | 11 | 10 |

Use the number line to help you.

Color all the 10's. How many do you see? _____

78

Direct students' attention to the addition square on page 78. Explain how to complete the number square.

### WRITE LEGIBLY

Before students write numerals in the squares, review how to write numerals 1–9. Remind students that numerals are tall and fill the space between the headline and baseline. Point out that numerals with two digits should be spaced close together but not touching.

After students write, go over their answers together.

Write the numerals from 1 to 9 in the boxes.

| 1 | 2 | 3 | 4 | 5 | 6 | 7 | 8 | 9 |
|---|---|---|---|---|---|---|---|---|

Finish the magic squares.
Each row across and down should add up to 15.
Each square should have every number from 1 to 9 in it.

| 4 | 9 | 2 |
|---|---|---|
| 3 | 5 | 7 |
| 8 | 1 | 6 |

| 1 | 9 | 5 |
|---|---|---|
| 6 | 2 | 7 |
| 8 | 4 | 3 |

79

Direct students' attention to the magic squares on page 79. Tell students that they will find it easier to complete a row where two numbers are shown. Explain that one way to check their work is to make sure every number from 1 to 9 appears in the magic square.

## COACHING HINT

For students having difficulty forming their numerals correctly, place on the chalk ledge a set of raised numerals made of seeds or sandpaper. Name a numeral. Have students take turns tracing the numeral several times as you say the stroke descriptions. (kinesthetic)

**A Numeral Survey**
Duplicate the questions below. Have students take the questions home and answer them.

*Which numeral tells your age?*
*Which numeral tells the day you were born?*
*Which numerals are on your house or apartment?*
*Which numerals do you see on telephone buttons (or dials)?*
*Which numerals do you see on a clock?*
(visual)

**Fun and Games**

**Spin, Clap, or Stamp**
Whisper a number to a student and ask that student to write the numeral on the chalkboard. If the student writes the numeral correctly, he or she can then give a direction for classmates to follow. Classmates must do the action the number of times indicated by the numeral on the board. Directions for actions might include the following: clap, stamp, spin, turn around, jump, bend, slide, march in place. (visual, kinesthetic)

## BEFORE WRITING

Read the jump-rope chant with students. Ask which words at the end of the lines rhyme *(pup, up)*. Ask students to suggest names for the pup that begin with each letter of the alphabet. Have students trace in the air the uppercase letter that begins each name as it is suggested. Ask a volunteer to write each letter on guidelines on the chalkboard. Focus on the letters and discuss their size and shape.

## FUN and GAMES

### Who Took My Bone?
For this version of "Doggie and the Bone," prepare bones from construction paper and place them along the chalk ledge. Choose one student to be the "dog" and sit in a chair with eyes closed. Choose another to take a bone, write a word on it, drop it under the dog's chair, and be seated. Then ask the dog to look at the bone and take three guesses as to who wrote the word. If the dog guesses correctly, he or she gets another turn. If not, the writer becomes the next dog. (visual)

---

**Size and Shape**
## Review

What shall I name
my little pup?
I'll have to think
a good name up.
Start with letter A.

> Pay special attention to size and shape.

Write the poem in your best handwriting.

> Circle your best word.

---

## WRITE LEGIBLY

Before students write, remind them to pay attention to their use of guidelines.

After students write, have them circle their best word and tell why they chose that word as their best.

## COACHING HINT

Encourage students to make retraces smoothly, in one continuous motion. Remind them that retraces go back over the same line. Have students practice retracing lines using colored pencils, markers, or crayons. (kinesthetic, visual)

## Keys to Legibility: Slant

Let's look at slant again.

Here's a good way to check your letters.
Draw lines through the pull down straight strokes.

 blueberries

If the lines you drew stand up straight, your word has correct slant.

bananas  strawberries

Write these words. Draw lines to check your slant.

I like apple pie.

Write this sentence. Draw lines to check your slant.

> Are your letters straight up and down?

81

---

## KEYS TO LEGIBILITY: SLANT

In the pages that follow, students concentrate on correct slant and evaluate their writing for this quality.

### MODEL THE WRITING

Model drawing lines through the pull down straight strokes in letters. Write the word *grapes* on the chalkboard. Draw lines over the pull down straight strokes in the letters **g, r, a,** and **p**. Remind students that writing letters straight up and down, with correct slant, will help make their writing easy to read.

### EVALUATE

like

To help students evaluate the slant of their letters, ask questions such as these:
Look at the word *like*. Are the pull down straight strokes in **l, i,** and **k** straight up and down?
Look at the word *pie*. Are the pull down straight strokes in **p** and **i** straight up and down?

### COACHING HINT

At the chalkboard, a left-handed student should stand a little to the right of his or her writing and pull the downstrokes toward the left elbow. The elbow is slightly bent, and the writing is done at a comfortable height on the chalkboard (between eyes and chin). As the writing progresses across the board, have the student move to the right to keep the downstrokes vertical. (kinesthetic)

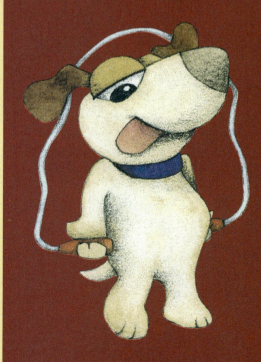

Read the following poem to your students.

**The Wishing Tree**
Imagine a tree
That grows so high
Its leaves and branches
Nearly touch the sky.
It's covered with fruits
Of every kind—
And I can pick them,
And no one will mind.

Begin a discussion about fruit trees by having students name and describe fruits that grow on trees.

Then share these facts about fruits:

Fruits are the edible parts of plants that contain the seeds. Fruits contain large amounts of water, but they also provide essential minerals and vitamins. Today almost every kind of fruit grows somewhere in North America.

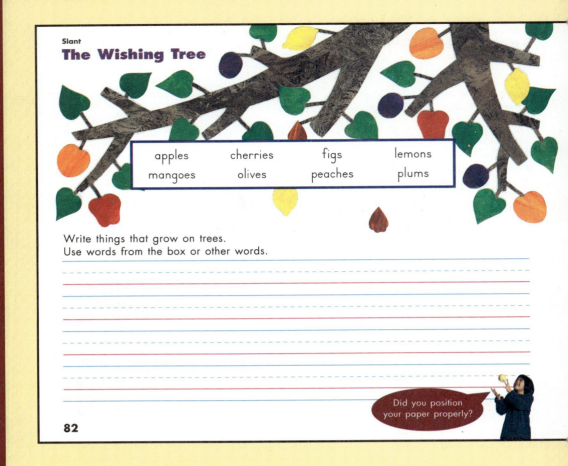

Slant
**The Wishing Tree**

| apples | cherries | figs | lemons |
|---|---|---|---|
| mangoes | olives | peaches | plums |

Write things that grow on trees.
Use words from the box or other words.

Did you position your paper properly?

82

## EVALUATE

Remind students that holding their pencil correctly and placing their paper in the right position will help them write letters straight up and down. Suggest they look at the slant of their letters.

To help students evaluate their writing, ask them to focus on one word at a time and ask questions such as these:
Look at the word *apples*. Are the pull down straight strokes in **a, p,** and **l** straight up and down?
Look at the word *lemons*. Are the pull down straight strokes in **l, m,** and **n** straight up and down?

## SLANT

To help students improve the vertical quality of their letters, have them practice writing pull down straight strokes on guidelines. Mark the starting point with a dot. Have them practice pull down straight strokes beginning at the headline or midline and ending at the baseline or next headline.

## On Your Own

What do you wish would grow on a tree?
Draw a picture and write about it.

Circle a word in which
your letters are straight up
and down.

83

## WRITE LEGIBLY

Before students write, remind them to check the position of their paper and pencil.

After students write, have them circle a word and tell which letters in the word were written with pull down straight strokes.

## COACHING HINT

Holding the pencil too tightly is a common problem that causes students to tire easily when writing. To overcome this problem, have the student crumple a piece of paper, place it in the palm of the writing hand, and pick up the pencil. This will serve as a reminder not to squeeze the pencil. (kinesthetic)

### A Wishing Tree

Read the folk tale *The Three Wishes* and discuss problems the characters faced when they were making their wishes. Then use construction paper to make a wishing tree for your class and display it on a bulletin board. Distribute drawing paper, and ask students to draw a leaf for the tree and to cut it out. Ask them to write on each leaf something they wish would grow on trees. Display the leaves on the tree and compare the kinds of things students wished for. (visual)

teddy bears

ice skates

### Make a Word Tree

Bring in a tree branch and set it up in a planter or bucket. Distribute index cards on which students can tape guidelines. With the students, choose a category of words for the tree. Have students write words on cards and use yarn to hang the cards on the tree branches. Continue the activity, using a new category each week. (visual)

Chant or sing this familiar verse with your students.

Oats, peas, beans, and barley grow.
Oats, peas, beans, and barley grow.
Neither you, nor I, nor anyone knows
How oats, peas, beans, or barley grows.

Begin a discussion on gardening. Encourage students to describe their personal experiences with home vegetable or flower gardens.

Explain that we eat different parts of plants. Tomatoes, cucumbers, peas, and eggplants are fruits of the plant. Lettuce is leaves. Carrots and radishes are roots. Celery stalks are stems, and cauliflower and broccoli are flowers.

**84**

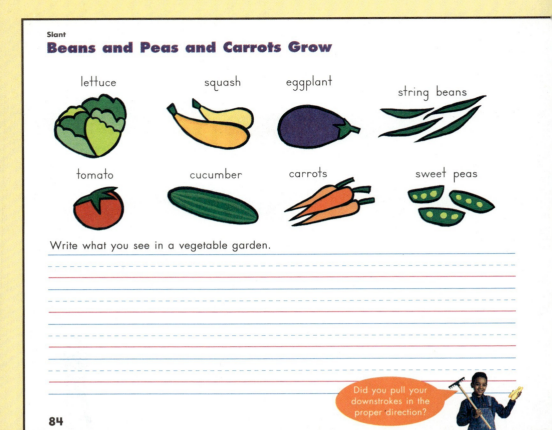

Slant
## Beans and Peas and Carrots Grow

lettuce    squash    eggplant    string beans

tomato    cucumber    carrots    sweet peas

Write what you see in a vegetable garden.

Did you pull your downstrokes in the proper direction?

84

## EVALUATE

Remind students that making pull down straight strokes straight is important for writing letters correctly. Suggest they look at their letters with pull down straight strokes.

beans

To help students evaluate the slant of their letters, ask them to focus on one word. Then ask questions such as these:
Which of your letters have pull down straight strokes?
Are your pull down straight strokes straight up and down?
Do your letters touch the correct guidelines?

## SLANT

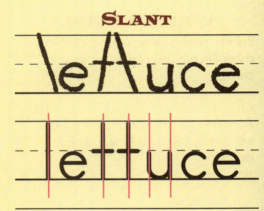

lettuce

lettuce

To help students improve the vertical quality of their letters, have them draw lines over the pull down straight strokes. If all the lines are parallel, the vertical quality is correct.

## On Your Own

Tell how you would plant a vegetable garden.

Circle a word in which your letters are straight up and down.

85

**Ads for Vegetables**

Provide poster paper for students to make a large poster advertising a certain fruit or vegetable. Suggest they emphasize taste and health benefits. Have them use crayons or markers to make a "delicious" picture and to add advertising copy to encourage their audience to try some. (visual)

# Fun and Games

**Make a Game Board**

Have groups of students work cooperatively to make vegetable and flower garden game boards. On oak tag, have them draw a winding path of squares. Around the path, have them draw and label vegetables and flowers. To play, students roll a die and move markers, such as seeds or pebbles, along the path from one side of the garden to the other. The winner is the first to move to the other side. (visual)

## WRITE LEGIBLY

Before students write, remind them to pay attention to pulling downstrokes in the right direction so their letters will be straight up and down.

After students write, have them circle a word with correct slant and tell which letters in the word have pull down straight strokes.

## HANDWRITING AND THE WRITING PROCESS

This page asks students to write directions. Explain that any process, such as baking a cake, has steps that must be followed in order. For prewriting, ask students to list steps for planting a garden, including a small drawing with each step. Drawing will help students focus on steps that are logical, complete, and in order.

To complete the writing process, have students revise and edit their drafts, checking spelling, punctuation, and handwriting. Have students publish their work by making pamphlets titled *How to Plant a Garden* to be made available in the school or local library.

## COACHING HINT

Help students recognize the improvement they have made in handwriting. Show them how to compare their current writing with samples from the beginning of the year. Such a comparison should provide motivation for further progress, particularly for students who have had difficulty with handwriting.

Read the following verse to your students while they look at the pictures on the page.

### Leaping Lizards

I have two lovely lizards.
Their home is a terrarium,
With sand and rocks, with
  twigs and plants;
They hide and climb and
  leap.
Their tails are long; their feet
  are short.
I love my leaping lizards!

Begin a discussion about lizards by sharing these facts:

Lizards can be kept as pets.

Skinks are among the smallest lizards. They grow to be about three inches long.

The largest lizard is the Komodo dragon, which can grow to about ten feet.

Invite children to share other information they know about lizards.

Slant
### Leaping Lizards

beaded lizard

six-lined race runner

blue-tongued skink

Write the name of each reptile.

Did you shift your paper as you wrote?

frilled lizard

86

## EVALUATE

Remind students that shifting the paper as they write will help them write letters with the straight up and down quality that produces good handwriting. Suggest they look at their letters for straight up and down quality.

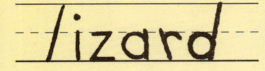

To help students evaluate the slant of their letters, ask them to compare their first and second writing of the word *lizard* and decide which one has the best straight up and down letters. Have them tell how they could improve any letters that are slanting.

## SLANT

lizard

To help students improve the vertical quality of their letters, prepare letters for them to write with the pull down straight stroke highlighted with a dotted line. Have students practice letters with a pull down straight stroke in this way.

## On Your Own
Make up a name for this lizard. Write about it.

Circle a word in which your letters are straight up and down.

### Leaping Lizards
Ask students to listen as you say the following alliterative phrases:

*leaping lizards*
*enormous eels*
*friendly frogs*

Ask what is alike about the words in each pair. Point out that one of the words names the animal and the other describes how the animal looks or acts. Ask students to work in pairs to write other alliterative phrases. Suggest they choose several to illustrate and label. Allow time for them to share their phrases. (auditory)

## FUN and GameS

### Paint a Letter
Place cards with the basic strokes in a bag near the chalkboard. Have students take turns choosing a card, naming the stroke shown, and writing a letter with that stroke on the board with a paintbrush and water. Ask volunteers to evaluate the writing before it dries. (kinesthetic, visual)

## WRITE LEGIBLY

Before students write, remind them to pay attention to the slant of their letters as well as the way they position their papers and pencils.

After students write, have them circle a word with correct slant and tell them to name a letter with pull down straight strokes.

Note: Illustration shows a flying dragon.

## HANDWRITING AND THE WRITING PROCESS

Thinking about legibility should always be part of the editing stage of the writing process. The **Keys to Legibility**—size and shape, slant, and spacing—help students know what to look for.

To check the slant of their writing, students can draw faint pencil lines through several vertical line letters on a draft and check to make sure the lines are parallel. As they look at their writing, students should ask themselves:
Is my writing straight up and down?
Do any letters slant left or right?

## COACHING HINT

Holding the writing instrument correctly affects handwriting quality. Students having difficulty with the conventional method of holding the writing instrument may wish to try the alternate method of placing the pencil between the first and second fingers.

Name the different hop-scotch games pictured and the country where each is played.

Invite students to describe each game pictured and tell which, if any, they have played.

Share these facts about hopscotch:

Hopscotch is a very old game originally played in England.

The name *hopscotch* includes its goal, which is to *hop* over the *scotch,* a line or scratch drawn on the ground.

Lines are drawn in various patterns, and the spaces are usually numbered so they can be hopped in order.

Variations of the game are played in many countries.

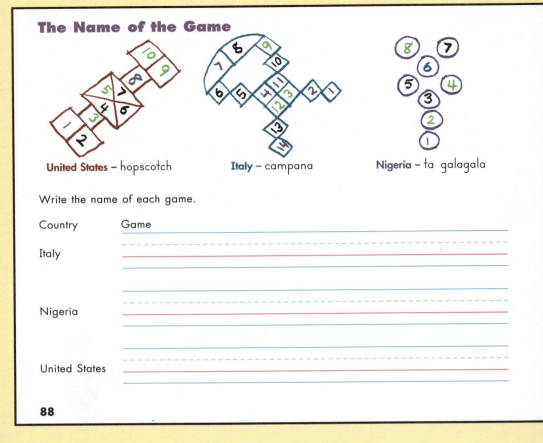

### The Name of the Game

**United States** – hopscotch     **Italy** – campana     **Nigeria** – ta galagala

Write the name of each game.

Country     Game

Italy

Nigeria

United States

88

## WRITE LEGIBLY

Remind students to write the names carefully.

After students write, you may wish to review the name given to each game and its country of origin.

*Practice Masters 72–90 provide practice in writing in Spanish.*

**Trinidad** – jumby

**France** – escargot

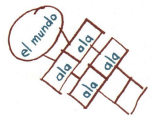
**El Salvador** – peregrina

Write the name of each game.

| Country | Game |
|---------|------|
| | |
| El Salvador | |
| | |
| France | |
| | |
| Trinidad | |

89

## COACHING HINT

Help students realize the importance of good handwriting in all subject areas. Provide writing activities for students to apply their handwriting skills.

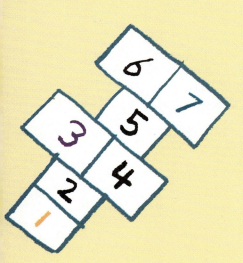

### Games We Play

Ask students to name and describe some of their favorite games. Write the following on the chalkboard.

Name:_____
Number of players:_____
How to play:_____
How to win:_____

Have students write the chart and complete it with information about a favorite game.

Ask students to share their information. (auditory, visual)

## **F**u**N** and **G**a**me**S

### Compound Word Challenge

Write *hopscotch* on the chalkboard. Ask what kind of word it is and elicit that it is a compound word. Then write *boat* on the board. Ask students to suggest two compound words that include the word *boat,* for example, *sailboat* and *rowboat.* Assign partners and ask students to write at least two compound words for each word you list on the chalkboard. Use this list to begin:

butter     air
snow       sun
water      bird

Share and compare completed lists. (visual)

## BEFORE WRITING

Read the poem on the page with students. Ask which words are repeated. Have students suggest other word pairs to replace *wiggle* and *waggle,* for example, *fiddle* and *faddle.* Recite the verse with each new suggestion.

## FᴜN and GᴀmeS

### Team Spelling

Line up students in two teams. Say a word students encounter frequently in their reading or use in their everyday writing. The first student on each team writes the first letter of the word on the chalkboard. Say the word again. The second student in each line writes the second letter. Continue until the word is completed. Check each letter for correct size and shape and slant. Give a point for each correctly written word. (auditory, visual)

---

Slant
### Review

Jelly in the bowl.
Jelly in the bowl.
Wiggle, waggle.
Wiggle, waggle.
Jelly in the bowl.

Pay special attention to slant.

Write the poem in your best handwriting.

Circle a word in which your letters are straight up and down.

90

## WRITE LEGIBLY

Before students write, remind them to pay attention to writing their letters straight up and down.

After students write, have them circle their best word and tell why they chose that word as their best.

## COACHING HINT

If students vary their line quality when they write, they may be holding their pencils too tightly, using their fingers to draw the strokes, tilting the pencils at different angles, or pressing too hard or too lightly with the pencils. Tell students to relax and check to see that they are holding their pencils correctly.

## Keys to Legibility: Spacing

Let's look at spacing again.

Look for letters and words that are too close or too far apart.
There should be enough space for an index finger to fit between words.

Sometimes I help at home.

Find the mistakes in each sentence. Write the sentences correctly.

I cleanmyroom.

I hang   up my cl ot hes.

I put   awaym yto ys.

Are your sentences easy to read?

91

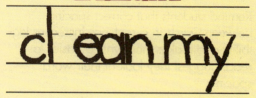

Write the following poem on chart paper and read it with students.

**Lend a Hand**
Oh, help me, little robot.
I've so very much to do.
Help me with my homework
And with the dishes, too.

Begin a discussion about how students help at home by asking them to name the chores they do. Extend the discussion to include ways students help at school.

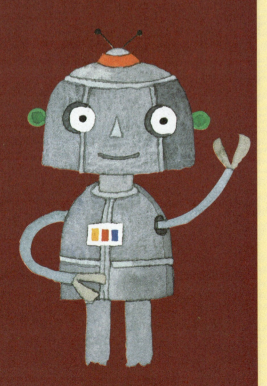

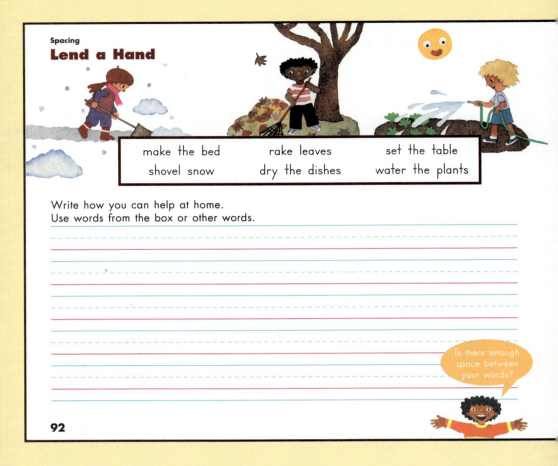

Spacing
## Lend a Hand

| make the bed | rake leaves | set the table |
| shovel snow | dry the dishes | water the plants |

Write how you can help at home.
Use words from the box or other words.

Is there enough space between your words?

92

## EVALUATE

Remind students that correct spacing between words in a sentence increases legibility and makes their writing easier to read. Suggest they look at their word spacing.

To help students evaluate their word spacing, have them focus on one of the chores they wrote. Then ask questions such as these:
Is there appropriate space between the words you wrote?
Is the space the same width between words?

## SPACING

To help students improve the spacing of their words, remind them to leave a finger space between words.

**On Your Own**

If you had a robot, what would you want it to do to help you? Write about it.

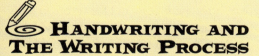

Put a star next to a sentence with good word spacing.

93

**Everyone Helps**

Invite students to write and complete the following sentence starters:

A teacher helps by_____.
The librarian helps by_____.
A fire fighter helps by_____.
My friend helps by _____.
I help by_____.

Then have students share their sentences.
(visual, auditory)

**Sort a Sentence**

For each group of four students, write a four-word sentence on a sentence strip. Cut the words apart and place them in a bag. Ask students to arrange the words to make a sentence. Have each of the four students write one of the words on the chalkboard to complete the sentence. Score one point for getting the words in the right order, one point for good spacing between words, and one point for good spacing between letters in a word. Students can exchange bags and play several times.
(visual, kinesthetic)

## WRITE LEGIBLY

Before students write, remind them to pay attention to the spacing of their words.

After students write, have them put a star beside a sentence with good word spacing and tell why they chose that line as their best.

## HANDWRITING AND THE WRITING PROCESS

Legible handwriting is important during every stage of the writing process. When publishing writing, it's especially important for students to use their best handwriting. Neat, legible writing shows courtesy to readers. It makes a good first impression, and it helps ensure that readers will understand the writer's message.

Encourage students to use their best handwriting as they publish their robot writing by making posters, picture books, or a bulletin board display.

## COACHING HINT

The more students practice handwriting, the easier it will be for them to use the correct spacing between words in a phrase or sentence. During handwriting time, provide some practice in sentence writing. You may want to have a space at the chalkboard for writing a sentence of the day for students to use as a model.

Write the following rhyme on chart paper and read it with your students.

Let's make a time capsule!
What shall we put in?
Buttons, books, and banners,
A baseball card, and a pin.

Begin a discussion about time capsules by exploring the idea that things are put into a time capsule which is then hidden or buried somewhere. Years later someone may discover it and learn about what was important to people in the past.

Invite students to imagine they have found a time capsule that was buried one hundred years ago. What things do they think would be in the capsule?

Spacing
### It's About Time

teddy bear
sunglasses
comic book
game
photo album
baseball card
newspaper
roller skate

Write what you see in the time capsule.

Is there enough space between your words?

94

## EVALUATE

Remind students that the reader should easily recognize where one word ends and another begins. Suggest students look at their word spacing.

To help students evaluate their word spacing, ask them to focus on their writing of *teddy bear*. Then ask questions such as these:
Are the words too close together?
Are the words too far apart?
Are the words spaced correctly?

## SPACING

Write on guidelines the following sentences with errors in word spacing.

*I would put in some stickers. Then I would try to find an old baseball cap to put in. Some shiny pennies would be good, too.*

To help students improve their word spacing, have them point out the errors in the sentences and rewrite them correctly. Tell students that two finger spaces should be left between sentences.

**On Your Own**

Write what you would put in a time capsule.

> Put a star next to an example of good word spacing.

## WRITE LEGIBLY

Before students write, remind them to pay attention to word spacing.

After students write, have them put a star beside an example of good word spacing and tell why they chose that sentence as their best.

## ✎ HANDWRITING AND THE WRITING PROCESS

Thinking about legibility should always be part of the editing stage of the writing process. The **Keys to Legibility**—size and shape, slant, and spacing—help students know what to look for.

To check their drafts for spacing, students can make sure there is about a one-finger space between words and about a two-finger space between sentences. Students should ask themselves:
Are my letters too close or too far apart?
Did I leave margins on my paper?
Did I indent each paragraph?

## COACHING HINT

Students can use a craft stick or a paper clip to help them check the spacing between words in a sentence. If a craft stick or paper clip will fit between their words, they have used correct spacing.

## Write Away

### Back in Time
Help students brainstorm a list of things we use today that people who lived about a hundred years ago did not have. After the list is on the chalkboard, have students work with partners to rewrite it in alphabetical order. Ask students to take home the lists and ask family members to add items. Invite students to share their completed lists. (auditory, visual)

## Fun and Games

### Design a T-Shirt
Give students a construction paper cutout of a T-shirt. Ask them to imagine that the T-shirt will be placed in a time capsule. Have them plan what message or design they would like to share with the people of the future and to write it on the T-shirt, using their best writing. (kinesthetic, visual)

Write the following poem on chart paper and read it with your students.

**Under the Sea**
How amazing it must be
To live all your life under the
    sea.
So far to travel, so far to
    roam,
With a great big ocean to
    call your home.

Begin a discussion about life under the sea by sharing these facts:

Water covers about two thirds of the earth. The sea is home to a vast variety of life. Fish are one kind of sea life. Plants and mammals also make their home there.

Invite students to share information about other sea animals.

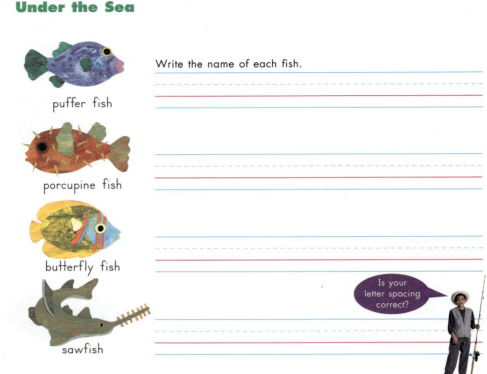

Spacing
## Under the Sea

puffer fish

porcupine fish

butterfly fish

sawfish

Write the name of each fish.

Is your letter spacing correct?

96

## EVALUATE

Remind students that writing words with correct letter spacing is important for legible handwriting. Suggest they look at their letter spacing in words.

# sa wfish

To help students understand correct letter spacing, write on the chalkboard several words with incorrect spacing. Ask questions such as these:
Which letters have the correct amount of space between them?
Which letters are too far apart?
Which letters are too close together?
Have students use these questions to evaluate the words they wrote.

## SPACING

Write the following sentences on guidelines, showing errors in word spacing.

*I think a good name for this fish would be crayon fish. It reminds me of my crayon box because it has so many colors.*

To help students improve their word spacing, have them point out the errors in the sentences and rewrite them correctly. Remind students that two finger spaces should be left between sentences.

## On Your Own

Make up a name for this fish. Write a story about it.

> Put a star next to a sentence with good letter spacing.

## WRITE LEGIBLY

Before students write, remind them to pay attention to the spacing between letters, words, and sentences.

After students write, have them put a star beside a sentence with good letter spacing and tell why they chose that sentence.

Note: Illustration shows parrot fish.

## ✎ HANDWRITING AND THE WRITING PROCESS

This page asks students to write a story. For prewriting, have students spend a few minutes imagining what they will write. Students can rehearse their stories by telling them to a partner. Encourage partners to ask questions that help the writer fill in missing details.

To complete the writing process, have students revise and edit their drafts, checking spelling, punctuation, and handwriting. Partners can work together to make fish-shaped mobiles that illustrate the stories. Publish the final versions by suspending them from the mobiles in your classroom.

## COACHING HINT

Use a prerecorded tape of letter names and stroke descriptions and provide an audiocassette tape player. Have students who still need practice with individual letters listen to the tape and write the letters described. (auditory, kinesthetic)

## Write Away

### Under the Sea ABC

Have students work in small groups to make Under the Sea ABC books. Distribute booklets with lined paper, one page for each letter of the alphabet. Provide research materials. Have students follow these steps.

1. Print an uppercase and a lowercase letter on each page.
2. Brainstorm an idea for it.
3. Write a sentence or phrase.
4. Illustrate the idea.

Here are ideas to get started:

Aa Animals everywhere
Bb Butterfly fish swimming
Cc Crabs crawling
Dd Dolphins rising for air
Ee Electric eels sliding
Ff Flying fish jumping
Gg Gray whales feeding
(visual, auditory)

## Fun and Games

### A Fishy Story

Read aloud a book about fish, such as *Swimmy*, by Leo Lionni. Ask students to retell the story in their own words. Have them draw and label a portrait of Swimmy. (auditory, visual)

## BEFORE WRITING

Ask students to join in as you say the verses of the jump-rope chant on pages 98 and 99. Have students jump to the rhythm and act out the verses. Then repeat the verses together and ask which words rhyme in each verse of the poem. Invite suggestions for changing lines two and four and recite them using students' suggestions.

Ask students to tell about their own teddy bears or to name their favorite bear characters from stories.

### Review

Teddy bear, teddy bear,
Turn around.
Teddy bear, teddy bear,
Touch the ground.

Teddy bear, teddy bear,
Show your shoe.
Teddy bear, teddy bear,
That will do.

Write a word that has three tall letters.

Write a word that has all short letters.

Write the word will.
Make sure the letters are straight up and down.

Write a six-letter word with correct letter spacing.

98

Review the directions with students before they complete the page.

When students have completed the page, you may wish to go over the answers together.

Teddy bear, teddy bear,
Turn out the light.
Teddy bear, teddy bear,
Say good night.

Pay attention to size and shape, slant, and spacing.

Write this verse in your best handwriting.

Put a star next to your best line of writing.

99

## WRITE LEGIBLY

Before students write, ask them to name the keys to legibility: size and shape, slant, and spacing. Ask volunteers to name some things to remember about each.

After students write, have them put a star next to their best line of writing, and tell why they chose that line as their best.

## COACHING HINT

Students who still have difficulty with correct letter size should continue to use paper with guidelines. Students who write on paper without guidelines can check their letter size by using a ruler to draw a horizontal line along the tops of the letters. (visual, kinesthetic)

## Write Away

### Teddy Bear Antics

Draw a web on the chalkboard. In the center, write the words *Teddy Bear.* Ask students to name things a teddy bear in a story might do, and add their ideas to the web. When the web is completed, ask students to write a story about a teddy bear. (auditory, visual)

## FuN and Games

### Rhyme and Write

Prepare enough cards so each student will have one. Write these words from the chant on the cards: *bear, turn, ground, light, out, say.* Distribute the cards and ask students to write as many words as they can that rhyme with the printed word. Have students read aloud their rhyming words and ask classmates to suggest words and add them to their lists. (auditory, visual)

## BEFORE WRITING

Invite students to share what they have accomplished in handwriting. Help them describe their progress in writing letters with correct size and shape, slant, and spacing.

Share the verse on the page with your students. Remind students that they wrote this verse at the beginning of the year. Explain that they will be writing the same lines today. Remind students to use correct letter size and shape, slant, and spacing as they write.

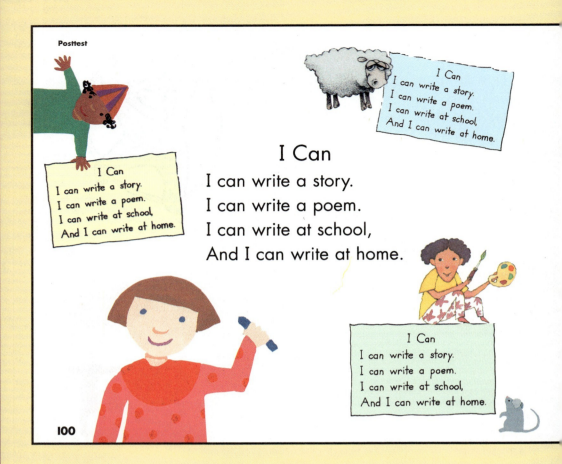

I Can
I can write a story.
I can write a poem.
I can write at school,
And I can write at home.

I Can
I can write a story.
I can write a poem.
I can write at school,
And I can write at home.

## I Can

I can write a story.
I can write a poem.
I can write at school,
And I can write at home.

I Can
I can write a story.
I can write a poem.
I can write at school,
And I can write at home.

100

## EVALUATE

Observe the students as they write. Then guide them in using the keys to legibility to evaluate their writing. Help them compare this writing to the writing on the pretest, and discuss how their writing has changed or improved. Meet individually with students to help them assess their progress.

Certificates of Progress *should be awarded to those students who show notable handwriting progress and* Certificates of Excellence *to those who progress to the top levels of handwriting proficiency.*

## I Can
I can write a story.
I can write a poem.
I can write at school,
And I can write at home.

Write the poem in your best handwriting.
Pay attention to size and shape, slant, and spacing.

Put a star next
to your best line
of writing.

101

## Brainstorm Ideas for Writing
Invite students to contribute ideas for topics they would like to write about. Include ideas for nonfiction and fiction. Organize the ideas on chart paper, and display the chart in your writing center. When students have free time, encourage them to choose a topic to write about and illustrate. (visual, kinesthetic)

### Ideas For Writing
Dinosaurs
Summer Vacation
Adventures
My Best Friend
The Circus

## Fun and Games

### Categories Anyone?
Play a game of categories using *HANDWRITING* as the basis for naming things. Write *HANDWRITING* down the left side of the chalkboard. Have students write it on lined paper, using one letter per line. Then ask them to write a word for each letter in a given category. For example, if the category is food, their list might begin like this:
*H is for ham.*
*A is for apple.*
(visual, kinesthetic)

The Record of Student's Handwriting Skills serves to indicate each student's progress in mastering the skills presented. The chart lists the essential skills in the program. After the skills that are listed have been practiced and evaluated, you will be able to mark the Record of Student's Handwriting Skills for either *Shows Mastery* or *Needs Improvement*.

## Record of Student's Handwriting Skills

### Manuscript

| | Needs Improvement | Shows Mastery |
|---|---|---|
| Positions paper correctly | ☐ | ☐ |
| Holds pencil correctly | ☐ | ☐ |
| Writes pull down straight lines | ☐ | ☐ |
| Writes slide right and slide left lines | ☐ | ☐ |
| Writes circle lines | ☐ | ☐ |
| Writes slant lines | ☐ | ☐ |
| Writes l and **L** | ☐ | ☐ |
| Writes i and **I** | ☐ | ☐ |
| Writes t and **T** | ☐ | ☐ |
| Writes o and **O** | ☐ | ☐ |
| Writes a and **A** | ☐ | ☐ |
| Writes d and **D** | ☐ | ☐ |
| Writes c and **C** | ☐ | ☐ |
| Writes e and **E** | ☐ | ☐ |
| Writes f and **F** | ☐ | ☐ |
| Writes g and **G** | ☐ | ☐ |
| Writes j and **J** | ☐ | ☐ |
| Writes q and **Q** | ☐ | ☐ |

102

## SHOWS MASTERY

Mastery of written letterforms is achieved when the student writes the letters using correct basic strokes. Compare the student's written letterforms with the letter models shown in the book. Keep in mind the keys to legibility (size and shape, slant, and spacing) when evaluating letters, numerals, words, and sentences for mastery of skill. Observation will indicate whether a student has mastered such skills as pencil and paper positions.

Check the appropriate box for each skill.

## NEEDS IMPROVEMENT

If a student has not mastered a skill, provide additional basic instruction and practice. First, determine the student's specific needs. Then return to the initial teaching steps of the lesson for ways to help the student. To improve letterforms, have the student practice writing the letter in isolation and within words and sentences. Reinforce instruction through activities geared to the student's modality strengths. Ask the student to evaluate his or her writing with you. Reevaluate the student's writing following practice over time. When mastery of the skill is achieved, check *Shows Mastery*.

*The Record of Student's Handwriting Skills is reproduced on Practice Master 54.*

| | Needs Improvement | Shows Mastery |
|---|---|---|
| Writes numerals 1–10 | ☐ | ☐ |
| Writes **u** and **U** | ☐ | ☐ |
| Writes **s** and **S** | ☐ | ☐ |
| Writes **b** and **B** | ☐ | ☐ |
| Writes **p** and **P** | ☐ | ☐ |
| Writes **r** and **R** | ☐ | ☐ |
| Writes **n** and **N** | ☐ | ☐ |
| Writes **m** and **M** | ☐ | ☐ |
| Writes **h** and **H** | ☐ | ☐ |
| Writes **v** and **V** | ☐ | ☐ |
| Writes **y** and **Y** | ☐ | ☐ |
| Writes **w** and **W** | ☐ | ☐ |
| Writes **x** and **X** | ☐ | ☐ |
| Writes **k** and **K** | ☐ | ☐ |
| Writes **z** and **Z** | ☐ | ☐ |
| Writes with correct size and shape | ☐ | ☐ |
| Writes with correct slant | ☐ | ☐ |
| Writes with correct spacing | ☐ | ☐ |
| Regularly checks written work for legibility | ☐ | ☐ |

103

# Index